THE Language OF BUSINESS ENGLISH

Workbook

Also available:

Brieger, N. and S. Sweeney
   The Language of Business English

Other ESP titles of interest include:

Adamson, D.
   Starting English for Business*

Brieger, N. and J. Comfort
   Production and Operations*

Brieger, N. and J. Comfort
   Personnel*

Comfort, J. and N. Brieger
   Marketing*

Comfort, J. and N. Brieger
   Finance*

Brieger, N. and J. Comfort
   Language Reference for Business English

Brieger, N. and J. Comfort
   Early Business Contacts*

Brieger, N. and J. Comfort
   Developing Business Contacts*

Brieger, N. and J. Comfort
   Advanced Business Contacts*

Brieger, N. and J. Comfort
   Technical Contacts*

Brieger, N. and J. Comfort
   Social Contacts*

Brieger, N. and J. Comfort
   Business Issues

Brieger, N. and A. Cornish
   Secretarial Contacts*

Davies, S. *et al.*
   *Bilingual Handbooks of Business
   Correspondence and Communication*

Goddard, C.
   Business Idioms International*

McBurney, N.
   Tourism

Minkoff, P.
   Executive Skills*

Sneyd, M.
   International Banking and Finance*
   Accounting*
   Insurance*

St John, M.-J.
   Marketing
   Advertising and the Promotion Industry

*Includes audio cassette(s)

THE
Language OF
BUSINESS ENGLISH
Workbook

Nick Brieger and Simon Sweeney

Prentice Hall

New York   London   Toronto   Sydney   Tokyo   Singapore

PRENTICE HALL INTERNATIONAL ENGLISH LANGUAGE TEACHING

Acknowledgements

The authors would like to thank Isobel Fletcher de Tellez
for her eagle-eyed alertness to detail and fleet-footed attention
to deadlines.

Published 1997 by
Prentice Hall Europe
Campus 400, Spring Way,
Maylands Avenue, Hemel Hempstead,
Hertfordshire, HP2 7EZ

Typeset in Plantin
by Ken Vail Graphic Design, Cambridge
Printed and bound in Great Britain by
Bath Press Colour Books

Library of Congress Cataloguing-in-Publication Data
Details are available on request from the publisher.

British Library Cataloguing in Publication Data
A catalogue record for this book is available from the
British Library.

ISBN 0–13–243007–X

4 3 2 1 99 98

◆ CONTENTS

v

CONTENTS

INTRODUCTION

Targets and objectives

The Language of Business English Workbook has been written in response to the request for more practice material in the grammar and functions of Business English. Like its companion volume, *The Language of Business English*, it is aimed at students who need to extend and practise the type of language used in professional situations. However, our special aim with this book has been to compare and contrast selected language forms so that learners can extend the accuracy and appropriacy of their language use.

The Language of Business English Workbook has been written specifically as an addition to *The Language of Business English* which contains reference material on grammar and functions. However, this book can be used together with any Business English course book to provide supplementary exercises in the grammar and functions of Business English. It is suitable for both classroom and self-study use.

Organisation of material

There are 84 units:
Units 1–64   Grammar
Units 65–84   Functions

Each unit is cross-referenced to the appropriate reference units in *The Language of Business English* (LOBE) so that learners can, if necessary, study the language forms being practised.

Each unit consists of controlled exercises to develop an awareness of the language forms and guided exercises to practise the range of meanings conveyed by these forms.

Answers to the controlled and guided exercises are given in the Key.

Selection of material

The book may be used either in class or for self-study. For classroom use, teachers should choose units to supplement the language areas covered by the Business English course book being followed, either to consolidate the presentation of language forms or to provide additional exercises. For self-study use, students should choose units according to their own interests or to problems they or their teachers have identified. For both teachers and students, the contents at the front of the book will help to locate appropriate units.

Using a unit

There are two types of exercises: controlled and guided.

Before you start an exercise:
- ◆ make sure you clearly understand the task;
- ◆ look at the relevant units of *The Language of Business English*, if necessary;
- ◆ complete the exercise.

After you have finished an exercise, check your answers with the Key at the back of the book.

Controlled exercises have only one possible solution; guided exercises have a model answer shown by (M). If your answers to a controlled exercise are wrong, look again at the relevant reference section(s) in the *The Language of Business English*. If your answers to a guided exercise are different to those suggested, check if your answers are possible alternatives. If you are not sure, then ask your teacher.

PART 1

GRAMMAR

See LOBE:
Unit 1 – The present continuous
Unit 2 – The present simple

Exercise 1

Are the following sentences right or wrong? If wrong, then correct them.

1 What exactly do you do in your job?
2 I am working for ABC in the accounts department.
3 How often do you carry out market research?
4 At present we are launch a new market campaign.
5 The company starts to export to other countries.
6 How many new products do you launch each year?
7 Our future is depending on the new financial team.

Exercise 2

Complete the following dialogue at a computer company's reception by putting the verbs in brackets into the correct tense.

Richard: How _____ you _____ (do)? My name _____ (be) Richard Li.

Isabel: Pleased to meet you. I _____ (be) Isabel de Miguel.

Richard: So, where _____ you _____ (come) from?

Isabel: From Spain. I _____ (work) in the Madrid office.

Richard: So, I _____ (suppose) that you _____ (work) on the new IT project.

Isabel: That's right. But how _____ you _____ (know) about the project? We _____ (try) to keep it confidential.

Richard: Yes, I _____ (know). But we _____ (belong) to the same project team. In fact we _____ (carry out) the same trials at the moment.

Isabel: Really. Well, how many people _____ your project _____ (involve)?

Richard: I'm afraid I _____ (not know). In fact no-one _____ (know). It's confidential at the moment!

Exercise 3

The Product Manager of a software company is giving a presentation. Select the most appropriate verb from the box below and put it into the correct present tense form.

Good morning, ladies and gentlemen. My name _____ Gilles Latour. I _____ in the marketing department as a product manager. In this short presentation I _____ to cover three main points. Firstly, the company's major activities; secondly, our present product range; and finally our future plans. If you _____ any questions, please _____ to ask.

As you _____, we _____ in customised software. Our clients _____ major corporations on both sides of the Atlantic. We typically _____ our activities into control systems and multimedia applications. At present the market for the latter _____ substantially. And for the former, we _____ to see an increase in the near future. We _____ some 250 people at our site in Newtown. And currently we _____ engineers for a new project for a Central European client. In addition to the permanent workforce, the company regularly _____ consultants at the customers' sites. They _____ us in areas such as installation and testing. OK, that _____ the first point. Now _____ us move on to the products in more detail.

be	not hesitate	look for	cover	include	not expect
divide	increase	specialise	employ	intend	use
help	know	work	have	let	

THE PAST CONTINUOUS versus THE PAST SIMPLE

See LOBE:
Unit 3 – The past simple
Unit 4 – The past continuous

Exercise 1

Combine a clause from the left with a clause from the right to make five sentences.

1	We were developing a new campaign	**a**	sales increased rapidly last year.
2	While the wage negotiations were continuing,	**b**	their competitors were launching their new product.
3	At the same time as they were testing their new products	**c**	the new director was planning cost-cutting measures.
4	Just as the financial director was making his retirement speech,	**d**	when we heard news of a takeover bid.
5	As I was saying a few minutes ago,	**e**	the workers started planning strike action.

Exercise 2

Complete the following extract from a letter to an advertising agency from the Sales Director of Supremo Supermarket by circling the correct form from the choice given.

Dear Paul
I **wrote/was writing** to you at this time last year to inform you of the developments in our company. At that time, we **negotiated/were negotiating** with the French company Hypervend for a share of the supermarket business. Hypervend subsequently **accepted/were accepting** our proposal and our products **started/were starting** to appear on the shelves at the end of the year. However, some six months later we **found/were finding** that customers **bought/were buying** more and more rival French products. Hypervend's management **said/were saying** that we **didn't package/weren't packaging** our products for French consumers, who **moved/were moving** to lighter and more colourful designs. We therefore **asked/were asking** you to study French packaging tastes. As I **said/was saying** when you **completed/were completing** your study, we **felt/were feeling** that your approach **didn't get/wasn't getting** to the heart of the matter.
Therefore, when we **received/were receiving** your invoice, I was surprised to see

Exercise 3

David has applied for a job with a new cosmetics company. Complete his interview by putting the verbs in brackets into the correct past tense form.

Interviewer: So how long _____ you _____ (work) for Matthews?

David: Just over two years.

Interviewer: And what tests _____ you _____ (carry out) while you _____ (work) there?

David: I first _____ (investigate) their motivation problems.

Interviewer: And what _____ the results _____ (show)?

David: In fact, while we _____ (process) the results, the company _____ (decide) to stop the project. You see, at the same time, the company _____ (develop) a new working model. And they _____ (need) additional people to implement that programme.

Interviewer: I see. So _____ you _____ (move) on to that project?

David: Yes. But while we _____ (work) on that project, the European funds _____ (stop). So, that's when I _____ (decide) to leave.

UNIT ◆3◆

THE PRESENT TENSES: SIMPLE, CONTINUOUS and PERFECT

See LOBE:
Unit 5 – The present perfect simple
Unit 6 – The present perfect continuous
Unit 1 – The present continuous
Unit 2 – The present simple

Exercise 1

Are the following sentences right or wrong? If wrong, then correct them.

1 What exactly do you do in your job?
2 Since when are you working for ABC?
3 So, when did you join the company?
4 I have been working for ABC since five years.
5 Last year we have introduced a new accounting system.
6 So far this year our results have been very satisfactory.
7 I have written this report all morning.
8 I'm afraid Mr Davison isn't in his office. He just went out.

Exercise 2

Complete the following introduction to a presentation by putting the verbs in brackets into the correct tense. You can choose from the present simple, present continuous, present perfect simple or present perfect continuous.

Good morning, ladies and gentlemen. My name is Martin Winkler and I _____ (work) in the R&D department here at Brymore. I _____ (work) on this current project for two years now. The project team _____ (consist) of myself and five engineers. Steven Brookes _____ (be) with us since the start of the project and he _____ (develop) the prototype which you'll see later. At present we _____ (test) the capacity of the prototype and we _____ (expect) to have some results later this month.

Now on to the presentation itself. I _____ (divide) it into three parts which I _____ (write) up here on this transparency. The first part _____ (cover) the project brief. The second part _____ (deal) with the team, who _____ (bring) special knowledge and skills to the project. And the third part _____ (look) at the project stages. As you'll see, other companies and institutes _____ (help) us and we are very grateful for their assistance.

Exercise 3

Combine a clause from the left with a clause from the right to make seven sentences.

1 I come from Spain,	a and now we are improving the features.
2 I've been working on this project for three years	b because the company hasn't increased its investment.
3 The project has been delayed,	c but I've been working in the UK for six years.
4 We have just completed the testing	d but now we are back on schedule.
5 We normally meet to discuss progress,	e so now are there any questions?
6 We are facing some problems	f and hope to complete it next year.
7 I've been talking for the last hour,	g but this week we haven't held a meeting.

THE PAST TENSES: SIMPLE, CONTINUOUS and PERFECT

See LOBE:
Unit 7 – The past perfect
Unit 3 – The past simple
Unit 4 – The past continuous

Exercise 1

The words in the following sentences are jumbled up. Put them into the correct order.

1 apply before building for had permission planning started to we we
2 while were we the the regulations planning hotel changed building
3 all completed explained formalities had that the we we
4 we the the said procedures hadn't followed correct authorities
5 bankrupt for of one our permission suppliers waiting we went were while
6 we tried to they had gone find bankrupt an alternative after

Exercise 2

Complete the following extract from a meeting by putting the verbs in brackets into the correct tense. You can choose from the past simple, past continuous or past perfect simple.

Jo: So what _____ you _____ (must) do before you _____ (start) the project?

Sarah: After we _____ (receive) the funding, we _____ (need) to prepare a detailed specification.

Jo: How long _____ that _____ (take)?

Sarah: Not long. After we _____ (assemble) the team, each member _____ (work) on their own part.

Jo: I see. And what _____ (happen) while everyone _____ (prepare) the specification?

Sarah: Nothing on this project. But everyone _____ (continue) to work on their other projects until everything _____ (be) ready. So, exactly three months after we _____ (receive) the funding, we _____ (begin) the investigation.

Jo: So when _____ the problems _____ (start)?

Sarah: One day, while we _____ (check) the equipment, we _____ (realise) that the computer _____ (not calculate) the right results since the beginning of the project.

Jo: I see. And do you know why the computer _____ (not work) properly?

Sarah: Not yet.

Exercise 3

Combine a clause from the left with a clause from the right to make five sentences.

1 While we were researching the chemical structure,	**a** we wrote a paper on it in a journal.
2 After we had found the molecule,	**b** they had discovered a similar substance earlier.
3 Once it had been identified,	**c** we found a new molecule.
4 We then waited some months	**d** until a pharmaceutical company approached us.
5 They explained in the meeting	**e** we needed to identify it.

UNIT 5

THE PRESENT TENSES and THE PAST TENSES

See LOBE:
Units 1–7 – The present and past tenses

Exercise 1

Are the following sentences right or wrong? If wrong, then correct them.

1   So what exactly do you do at Monroe Systems?
2   I am work in the Accounts Department.
3   And how long do you work there?
4   I have joined the company eight years ago.
5   And when did you start working in the Accounts Department?
6   I work there since four years.

Exercise 2

Complete the following sentences by putting the verbs into the correct present or past tense.

1   I am glad to report that sales _____ (increase) at present.

2   I really _____ (not understand) these figures. What _____ they
    _____ (mean)?

3   Last year we _____ (reduce) the workforce by 8 per cent.

4   At this time last year we _____ (enjoy) a big rise in sales.

5   _____ you _____ (read) this report on rationalisation yet?

6   We _____ (use) our present consultants for three years now.

7   The MD reported that the company _____ (have) good results in the previous quarter.

Exercise 3

Complete the following conversation at a reception by putting the verbs into the correct present or past tense.

Paul: How _____ you _____ (do)? My name _____ (be) Paul Roberts.

Andreas: Pleased to meet you. Mine's Andreas Schmidt.

Paul: I _____ (not think) we _____ (meet) before.

Andreas: No, I only _____ (join) the European firm nine months ago. Before that I
            _____ (work) out in Bangkok.

Paul: What _____ you _____ (do) out there?

Andreas: I _____ (manage) recruitment and selection for the South East Asian region.
            But then my wife _____ (say) that she _____ (not see) Europe for many
            years and that she _____ (want) to go back.

Paul: And _____ you _____ (agree)?

Andreas: Yes, of course. And _____ you _____ (be based) here in London?

Paul: No, actually I _____ (work) in Madrid, though I _____ (live) near
            London for many, many years. You _____ (see) I _____ (join) the
            Spanish office when I _____ (start) my career.

Andreas: But _____ your family _____ (not mind) you working away from home?

Paul: Well, actually my wife _____ (do).

Andreas: So what _____ (happen)?

Paul: Oh, we _____ (get) divorced some time ago.

6 UNIT

THE FUTURE FORMS

See LOBE:
Unit 8 – The future with **will**
Unit 9 – The future with **going to**
Unit 1 – The present continuous
Unit 2 – The present simple

Exercise 1

Complete the following dialogue by putting the verbs in brackets into the correct future form.

Don: When _____ the next training programme _____ (start)?

Bill: We _____ (run) the next one in January.

Don: And how many participants _____ (attend)?

Bill: I expect that we _____ (have) at least twenty.

Don: _____ you _____ (arrange) an evening programme?

Bill: Probably, yes, but in any case we _____ (review) the arrangements before the

         seminar. I _____ (send) you a copy of the programme, if you are interested.

Don: Thanks. When _____ the programme _____ (be) ready?

Bill: By the end of next month.

Exercise 2

Match the following questions (1–8) with the most appropriate answer (a–h).

1 What are you doing this evening?
2 When are you going to visit the office in Ankara?
3 What are you going to do if profits are down?
4 When can you send the information?
5 When does the meeting start?
6 How long are you staying in KL?
7 When will the first stage be finished?
8 Who else will be at the meeting?

a It says 9 o'clock in my programme.
b I expect we'll be ready to take the next step in about two months.
c I am definitely going to ask for his resignation.
d I think I'll see the whole team from New York.
e I don't know. I haven't decided yet. What about you?
f Just a couple of days.
g I'll do it right away.
h Some time later this year.

Exercise 3

Complete the following phone conversation by putting the verbs into the correct future form.

Johan: So when _____ you _____ (launch) the new product?

Henry: It's scheduled for next month, but we _____ (have to) make some changes.

Johan: And what about sales training?

Henry: We _____ (run) a series of workshops over the next two weeks.

Johan: Good. Look Henry, I _____ (visit) London next week. I'd like to come

         over and visit you.

Henry: When exactly _____ you _____ (be) in London?

Johan: My plane _____ (arrive) on Thursday at 2 o'clock.

Henry: Thursday afternoon's no good for me. What _____ you _____ (do) in

         the evening?

Johan: Nothing. I think I _____ (book) a table for us at the Brasserie. About 8?

Henry: Sounds great. See you there.

UNIT 7

THE CONDITIONALS (1)

See LOBE:
Unit 10 – The conditionals (1)
Unit 11 – The conditionals (2)

Exercise 1

Are the following sentences right or wrong? If wrong, then correct them.

1 If we increase productivity, we will remain profitable.
2 Provided we will remain profitable, we can invest in our plant.
3 Unless we invest in the plant, our competitors will overtake us.
4 If we would ask for a bank loan tomorrow, I'm sure we would get it.
5 If we had taken a loan two years ago, we could have secured our market position.
6 As long as interest rates remain high, banks are eager to find new business.
7 If the economy would remain stable, it would help industry.
8 If we would have known the scale of inflation, we could have reduced our running costs.

Exercise 2

Look at these instructions for safety procedures at a chemical factory. Combine a clause from the left with a clause from the right to make five sentences.

1 If you make an error,
2 If there was a serious error,
3 As long as the bell has been reset,
4 So, if you hear the alarm,
5 You mustn't re-enter the building,
6 Finally, if you want to know more about safety procedures,

a it will go off.
b unless the supervisor tells you.
c you will hear a warning signal.
d you can look in the manual.
e everybody must leave the building.
f the alarm would ring three times.

Exercise 3

Complete the following extract from a discussion by putting the verbs into the most suitable conditional form.

Chris: If we _____ (want) to recruit better workers, we need to offer better rates of pay.

Maria: I disagree. Just look at Mansell. If we _____ (follow) their example, we _____ (be) bankrupt by now. If we _____ (offer) the highest wages, I doubt that it would make us a better employer.

Chris: Well, look at it the other way round. If we don't attract better workers, we simply _____ (not get) the orders.

Maria: Why not?

Chris: Because of investment. If a company _____ (want) to succeed it must invest in all aspects of the business. And that includes the workforce.

Maria: So, if we were to invest in the workforce, how _____ you _____ (suggest) going about it?

Chris: I _____ (recommend) a study of the average wage in this area for different types of work. And then we should offer a competitive rate for different grades, as long as everyone _____ (agree).

Maria: And what if they _____ (not agree)?

Chris: Then Bob _____ (must) make the final decision.

See LOBE:
Unit 10 – The conditionals (1)
Unit 11 – The conditionals (2)

Exercise 1

Which type of conditional sentence (I, II or III) are the following equivalent to?

1 Had we known the details, we would have informed you.
2 Should we find out any further details, we will inform you.
3 Were we to get any further information, we would let you know immediately.

Exercise 2

Put the following sentences from a legal document into the correct order.

> Goods will be accepted as long as they are returned in the original packaging and in full working order. ( )
>
> Should a claimant wish to appeal against the decision of the commercial court, appeal may be made to a court of law. ( )
>
> The company shall not pay any costs in settling the dispute in any court unless the company has been negligent. ( )
>
> If a customer is dissatisfied with the goods, s/he may return them within 28 days and claim a full refund. ( )
>
> In case of any dispute under this contract, it shall first be presented at a commercial court. ( )
>
> Should a purchaser return the goods, all costs incurred in returning them shall be paid by the purchaser. ( )
>
> In the event that the company incurs any costs to prepare the goods for resale, these shall be deducted from the money to be repaid to the purchaser. ( )

Exercise 3

*Rewrite the following **if** constructions using the phrase shown in brackets and making any other necessary changes.*

1 *If you claim for injury, we will investigate it. (in the event of)*

   _____

2 *We can't carry out a full investigation if we don't have all the documentation. (unless)*

   _____

3 *If we require an external assessment, we will consult an expert. (inversion with 'should')*

   _____

4 *If you need the information, take a photocopy. (in case)*

   _____

5 *We will review your case, if you agree to bear any additional costs. (so long as)*

   _____

6 *If we changed our decision, we would reimburse all additional costs. (inversion with 'were')*

   _____

7 *If all papers have been received, we will settle all claims within 30 days. (provided that)*

   _____

8 *If you had made a fraudulent claim, we would have taken you to court. (inversion with past perfect)*

   _____

UNIT 9

TENSE REVIEW (1)

See LOBE:
Unit 12 – Tense review

Exercise 1

Are the following sentences right or wrong? If wrong, then correct them.

1 What exactly do you do in your job?
2 I am working for Manpower in the Personnel Department.
3 Do you work on any special projects at the moment?
4 What were you doing before you joined Manpower?
5 I was working for an international headhunting agency, when Manpower was recruiting me.
6 How long have you worked for Manpower?
7 When have you joined Manpower?
8 I work there since three years.
9 I've planned a series of assessment seminars. I will run the first one on 1 August.
10 I can't find the information at the moment. I will fax it to you later.
11 If I can't find the information today, I'll call you tomorrow.
12 If the dates of the assessment centres will be changed, I would let you know immediately.

Exercise 2

Put the following sentences from GloboPaint's prospectus into the correct order. Some of them have been done for you.

During the company's hundred-year history, the organisation has seen many changes in production techniques.(10)

Henry Hutchison, the company's chief executive officer, said at a recent meeting, 'GloboPaint is not going to stand still.' ( )

In fact, it is still expanding. ( )

As GloboPaint knows, if they don't invest in new processes they won't be able to compete. (12)

In fact, if they had not diversified, they would not have survived. ( )

So, initially they concentrated on just one product. ( )

The next generation of paints will be entirely produced by computer-controlled equipment. ( )

The original company, called Hammer Paints, was started by two brothers who were working as engineers. ( )

Their results showed that there was a clear need for more effective industrial paints. ( )

GloboPaint was established more than 100 years ago in a small workshop near Great Hammerton.(1)

They had done some market research before they set up Hammer Paints. ( )

Today it employs more than 5,000 people in a worldwide operation with offices in more than 30 countries. ( )

Today they manufacture a range of more than 250 paints as well as other oil-based products.(8)

Exercise 1

Daniela Stranb is applying for the job of marketing assistant. She has come by car from Germany to Switzerland. Look at her CV and complete the exchanges from the beginning and the middle of the interview, by writing appropriate questions to the answers given.

Daniela Straub
Grinzingerstr. 43
D-4896 Huppingen
GERMANY

EDUCATION
1984-93   Gymnasium Huppingen
           Specialised in French and English

PROFESSIONAL EXPERIENCE

Employer	Dates	Position and responsibilities
Spartia	1993-1994	Marketing Assistant: responsible for German clients. Left because no possibility of international career.
Copert	1994-	Assistant to International Marketing Director: support Director with international marketing activities, especially in England and France.

CURRENT CAREER OBJECTIVE
As there is no chance for me to progress in my present job, I would like to find a more challenging professional position and an opportunity to learn more about marketing.

I: _____ ?

DS: How do you do?

I: _____ ?

DS: Fairly quick. Not too much traffic.

I: _____ ?

DS: Just one and a half hours.

I: So, I'd like to ask you about your education first.

      _____ ?

DS: English and French.

I: _____ ?

DS: Yes, quite regulary in my last job at Copert.

I: _____ ?

DS: No, not at all. All our clients were in Germany.

I: _____ ?

DS: Because there was no possibility of an international career.

I: _____ ?

DS: Because they offered me a job in the international department.

I: _____ ?

DS: Because I don't think there is a chance for me to progress.

I: _____ ?

DS: Basically a challenge and the opportunity to learn more about marketing.

Exercise 2

Now complete the sentences from the end of the interview by putting the verbs into the correct form.

I: OK, Ms Straub, we _____ (conduct) interviews all week for this post. In fact, I _____ (interview) eight candidates already and I _____ (see) three more today and tomorrow. After we _____ (interview) all the candidates, we _____ (make) a quick decision and _____ (let) our first choice know by the end of next week. We _____ (intend) to have the whole process finished in two weeks' time. Now, if we _____ (offer) you the job, when _____ (can) you start?

DS: I _____ (need) to give one month's notice to my current employer and then, of course, I _____ (need) a little time to arrange a move here. Initially I _____ (can) commute.

I: _____ (you/have) any further questions at the moment?

DS: No, nothing else. You _____ (answer) all my questions.

I: Well, if you _____ (think) of anything else, _____ (not hesitate) to call me.

UNIT 11

VERB ...ING versus INFINITIVE (1)

See LOBE:
Unit 13 – Verb ...ing
Unit 14 – Infinitive

Exercise 1

Underline any mistakes in the following discussion. Then correct them.

Andreas: Are we ready to begin?

Bill: Yes, let's start. To think about the agenda, my view is it won't be possible to think about every point today. We should to concentrate on the main item.

Andreas: I'm prepared agreeing, if we all think that … it is the main item.

Cathy: The main thing, yes. Let's to concentrate on that.

Andreas: Right, that's agreed. By to leave the discussion of Crystal Brothers, we can to finish the main business.

Bill: Okay. Then I'd like to introduce the main discussion today.

Andreas: Er, yes, can I suggest to break for a coffee at 10?

Bill: Coffee! Good idea. Coffee at 10.

Cathy: Right, Andreas, it's not worth to go through the report in detail. We've all read it.

Andreas: Of course. I don't want to waste time reading it to you.

Exercise 2

Read the extract from an advertisement for Global Air, a Singapore-based airline. Choose the right form of the verb from the alternatives given.

 Travelling/To travel to America?

Global Air can take/to take you to over **100** American and Latin American cities, without you or your luggage to change/changing airline on the way. Don't risk missing/to miss your connections, avoid to complicate/complicating your trip. No other airline makes to fly/flying to America such a pleasure. Travel should be fun,

Global Air makes it wonderful.

Exercise 3

Fill in the spaces in the memo below. Use the correct form of the following verbs.

persuade   postpone   go   prepare   see   know

Internal Memo

Date: 10 May
From: TA
To: PF

Dear Paul,
I'd like _____ you later today. The MD
has suggested _____ to Japan next week.
I'm having difficulty _____ him that we
need more time _____ our presentation.
I'd appreciate _____ your views. Do you
think we should _____ the trip?

Trudy

VERB ...ING versus INFINITIVE (2)

See LOBE:
Unit 13 – Verb ...ing
Unit 14 – Infinitive

Exercise 1

Look at part of a letter to shareholders about a rights issue. Fill in the spaces with the correct form of the verbs below.

| raise | return | offer | hold | express | recommend | be | invest | guarantee |

Vida Assurance p.l.c.
Century House
10-16 City Road
London EC1 5TF
1 August 1995

Dear Shareholder,

As you may _____ aware from reports in the national media, the Board of Directors of Vida Assurance is planning _____ extra capital from existing shareholders through a rights issue. We recommend this option as the best way _____ the long-term security of the company. It is also our belief that the offer of additional shares will be an attractive investment, and we are sure you will agree it is worth _____ extra money in the company.

As is normal with rights issues, the shares will be available at a low price, _____ an excellent investment opportunity. In _____ them to you, we believe we have both the company's best interests and yours at heart.

Of course, the Board does not wish _____ a rights issue without the support of shareholders. We invite you _____ your views on this policy at an extraordinary general meeting on 24 October at the National Exhibition Centre, or by _____ the form enclosed with this letter.

Exercise 2

Read the following extract from a report on a meeting. Fill in the spaces with the right form of the verb in brackets.

Meeting Report

Meeting: 12 March 19.., Paris.
Subject: Distribution channels
Participants: FD, HF, GF, TR, SA, MF.

Summary

The preferred route for _____ (ship) our products to Europe is by air from Tokyo to London. We have successfully used this route for seven years. _____ (use) alternative routes in the past would have required more complicated distribution arrangements. Until now, our European distribution operations have centred on the UK. _____ (change) this does not seem appropriate at the moment, but we can _____ (look at) alternatives. It is certainly worth _____ (find out) the costs of _____ (open) a new distribution centre in southern Europe. We agreed _____ (set up) a committee _____ (investigate).

UNIT 13

VERB ...ING versus INFINITIVE (3)

See LOBE:
Unit 13 – Verb ...**ing**
Unit 14 – **Infinitive**
Unit 15 – Verb ...**ing** or infinitive + **to**

Exercise 1

Underline and correct three errors in the following internal memo.

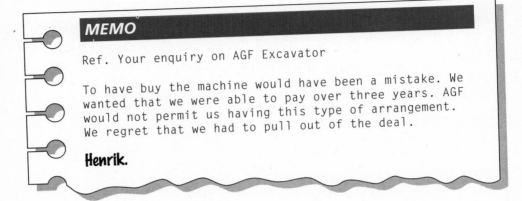

MEMO

Ref. Your enquiry on AGF Excavator

To have buy the machine would have been a mistake. We wanted that we were able to pay over three years. AGF would not permit us having this type of arrangement. We regret that we had to pull out of the deal.

Henrik.

Exercise 2

Read the discussion below about quality tests in a manufacturing company. Change the underlined phrases for one of the combinations given in the box, making any necessary grammatical changes.

| try/test   stop/think about   recall/have   stop/be |
| like/think   go on/introduce |

Pedro: Now, about these tests. We <u>attempted to test</u> the product last week but the machinery was faulty so the results were unreliable.

Bob: I <u>remember we had</u> a problem with this test last time.

Pedro: If we <u>were not</u> so worried about tests, we would develop new products more quickly.

Bob: On the contrary, I <u>think it's good to know</u> that we're very concerned about quality.

Pedro: If you <u>gave time to consider</u> how much money we spend on testing, you'd be shocked.

Bob: Not at all. So long as we <u>continue to make</u> new products, we'll carry on testing them.

Exercise 3

Complete the following telephone call.

S: Good morning, SAWA Enterprises.

A: Hello, I'd like _____ (speak) to Mr Hashimoto.

S: Who's calling, please?

A: Andreas Blöm, from Salzburg. I wonder if I could _____ (see) him this week?

S: I'm sorry, Mr Hashimoto is not free this week. He tried _____ (phone) you last week but you were in New York.

A: Yes, I'm sorry. I remember _____ (ask) him to call me, but I forgot _____ (tell) him I would be away.

S: Perhaps I can ask him _____ (call) you as soon as he is free next week.

A: Yes, please do. I'll look forward _____ (hear) from him.

S: Okay. Thank you for _____ (call). We'll talk again next week.

A: Fine. Bye for now.

S: Goodbye.

VERB ...ING OR INFINITIVE + TO versus VERB + OBJECT + INFINITIVE

See LOBE:
Unit 15 – Verb ...ing or infinitive + to
Unit 16 – Verb + object + infinitive

Exercise 1

Read the following sentences and decide which of the given meanings is the correct one.

1 During development, we stopped to think about the difficulties.
   a We stopped thinking about the difficulties and we don't think about them now.
   b For a short time, during the development, we did not think about the difficulties.
   c We did think about the difficulties during the development phase.
2 I like to call customers, to check that they are happy a few weeks after buying a machine from us.
   a I think it is a good policy to check that the customer is happy.
   b I really enjoy calling customers to check that they are happy.
   c I would like to call customers, to check that they are happy.
3 I was trying to contact Acorn last week.
   a I attempted to call Acorn last week.
   b I succeeded in contacting Acorn last week.
   c I did not attempt to call Acorn last week.
4 I remembered to include our price list with the letter.
   a I recall putting the price list in the envelope.
   b I sent the price list with the letter.
   c I forgot to send the letter.
5 We stopped to visit Mr Smith in Moscow.
   a We do not visit Mr Smith any more.
   b On a recent trip we interrupted our travels to visit Mr Smith in Moscow.
   c We did not visit Mr Smith when we were in Moscow.

Exercise 2

*Make five sentences using the words in the box below. Each sentence should contain either verb + object + infinitive, or verb ...**ing** or the infinitive.*

I asked	me	to accept	Kroll.
They allow	us	to see	a training programme.
They persuaded	him	to call	you yesterday.
I tried		running	their offer.
We suggest			a 10 per cent discount.

Exercise 3

Here is an extract from a telephone conversation. A Sales Manager is describing a meeting with a potential customer. Complete the spaces with appropriate endings from the box below.

They liked having an on-site demonstration and suggested _____ . They persuaded _____ . They wanted _____ . The last point was impossible for us. We did not expect _____ .

us to accept their payment terms	them to be so uncompromising
having the machine on trial	us to cut our price

UNIT 15

WILL, WOULD, SHALL, SHOULD (1)

See LOBE:
Unit 17 – **Will** and **would**
Unit 21 – **Shall** and **should**

Exercise 1

Here is a part of a conversation between two people about a meeting. Insert contractions where possible.

Marina: Do you think Kit will arrive during the day or in the evening?

Paul: He should be with you by mid-day.

Marina: Good. We will have lunch together. Shall I book a restaurant?

Paul: That would be nice.

Marina: Please ask him to ask for me at reception when he arrives.

Paul: I will tell him that, of course.

Marina: And tell him it would be good if he brought a copy of the Arrow report.

Paul: He should have sent it to you already.

Marina: Okay. Perhaps you would ask him to check.

Paul: I shall do that.

Exercise 2

*Chemco is a pharmaceuticals manufacturer. Here is an extract from the company newspaper about a new drug. Change the underlined parts to different verb forms using **will**, **would**, **shall** or **should**.*

The development phase of Arpanol ends on Friday this week. The next phase, licensing, <u>begins</u> next week. The final report on clinical trials <u>is probably going to</u> be finished this month. Of course we <u>are happy to</u> send a copy to all the laboratories who helped with the tests. The drug <u>is expected to</u> be licensed by the FDA early next year and, once licensed, <u>is going to</u> be sold internationally. It <u>is going to</u> be available in liquid and tablet form.

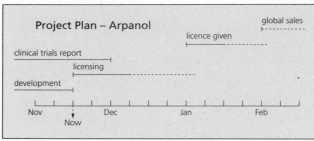

Project Plan – Arpanol

Exercise 3

*You are telling your sales team about new targets for the next season. Rewrite the sentences using **will**, **would**, **shall** or **should** as appropriate.*

1   I expect, in general, a 10 per cent increase on last year.
    There _____ a 10 per cent increase on last year.

2   If you like I can give you a written summary of the targets for each region.
    _____ you a written summary of the targets for each region?

3   The competition is definitely not going to be less than last year.
    The competition _____ than last year.

4   As a new initiative, I want you to send me a report at the end of each week.
    As a new initiative, I _____ .

5   We did not do this last year, which was a mistake.
    We _____ done this last year.

6   I think, but I'm not sure, that in the urban areas we are going to have a good season.
    _____ a good season in the urban areas.

WILL, WOULD, SHALL, SHOULD (2)

See LOBE:
Unit 17 – **Will and would**
Unit 21 – **Shall and should**

Exercise 1

Use **will, would, shall, should** in the following sentences.

1   Ask Paula for help in understanding the details of a contract.
'Paula, _____ explain the details of the contract to me?'

2   Offer to help Tom, a colleague, with a computing problem.
'_____ , Tom?'

3   Tell a colleague it is probably explained in the operating manual.
'It _____ manual.'

4   Suggest you arrange a meeting with Agos Ltd next week.
'_____ Agos next week?'

5   Offer a visitor a drink.
'_____ a drink of something?'

6   Tell a colleague that Down Inc. rejected your request for better terms. (use 'accept')
'They _____ .'

7   Advise a colleague to write to the supplier of a faulty machine.
'You _____ .'

8   Suggest what should be written on a notice telling visitors to report to Security on arrival.
'All visitors _____ on arrival.'

Exercise 2

Complete the following dialogue.

'Will John arrive this morning?'

'No, _____ _____ .'

'What about later today?'

'If the trains are running on time, he _____ _____ here after lunch.'

'Is Mary coming too?'

'No, she said she _____ _____ this time.'

'What about next month?'

'Yes, she _____ .'

'_____ I ask Henry to see John today?'

'Yes, he _____ see him, I think.'

Exercise 3

Rewrite the following dialogue using **will, would, shall** or **should** in every sentence.

Wilhelm: Is the packaging design going to be different from the old one?

Jake: Yes – and the machine is going to have to be modified.

Wilhelm: Do you want me to do that?

Jake: No, my advice is to get Abacus to do it. They offered to do it.

Wilhelm: Isn't that going to be expensive?

Jake: No, I don't think so.

UNIT ◆17◆
MAY, MIGHT, CAN, COULD

See LOBE:
Unit 18 – **May** and **might**
Unit 19 – **Can** and **could**

Exercise 1

Label the following as present possibility (PP), future possibility (FP), request for permission (RP), prohibition (P), ability (A).

1 May I use your telephone?
2 There may be an upturn in our overseas sales next year.
3 There might be delays between here and the airport.
4 Can you finish the study before we meet next week?
5 You can't telephone out with that line.
6 Administrative staff may not authorise payments above a certain limit.
7 We couldn't convince him to abandon the idea.

Exercise 2

Underline and correct any mistakes in the following interview between a journalist and a Finance Minister.

Journalist: May I ask, Minister, are you concerned about the rise in inflation to 3 per cent?

Minister: Naturally, but I think you can be surprised by the new unemployment figures that come out next week.

Journalist: But, can I ask you about inflation? Might there be a further rise next month?

Minister: Economics is not a science like physics or chemistry. It is possible, there can be a rise next month too.

Journalist: Might you tell me, what annual inflation figure do you now expect?

Minister: As I have said before, I mightn't make a guess on this.

Journalist: But you are the Finance Minister!

Minister: Yes, but may I repeat, economics is not an exact science.

Exercise 3

Read the following extract from a newspaper report on a takeover in the car industry. Change the underlined phrases to include **may**, **might**, **can** or **could**.

ASA job cuts threat

The takeover of ASA Autos by Dawa is likely to mean job losses at ASA's main production plants in Europe. A spokesperson for Dawa said it was too early to be certain, but some redundancies are a possibility. It is possible however that the company will increase its small car production in Europe. Dawa are not able to meet demand for their small cars in the Far Eastern markets, so this is an obvious area where they will probably expand their activities. Industry analysts think there is a small possibility of another major takeover in the car market soon.

MAY, MIGHT, CAN, COULD, MUST, MUSTN'T, NEEDN'T

See LOBE:
Unit 18 – **May** and **might**
Unit 19 – **Can** and **could**
Unit 20 – **Must, mustn't** and **needn't**

Exercise 1

Mark the following sentences as future possibility (FP), ability (A), request for permission (RP), obligation (O), prohibition (P), logical deduction (D), no necessity (NN).

1 The company must expand its operations overseas.
2 We couldn't market Gajo in the USA as we had no export licence.
3 Can the Marketing Department be responsible for the licence application?
4 We needn't apply for an export licence for every product.
5 We may have problems selling the Fano range in Japan.
6 Could I see a copy of the report on Fano marketing in the USA?
7 You must have seen it already – everyone had a copy.

Exercise 2

There are six modals in the following exchange between two technicians in a food processing plant. There is a mistake with each one. Correct them.

A: We must to check the temperature control on the mixing unit.

B: No, we mustn't do that. It must had been checked already. It's the first thing to look at.

A: Then it can have been faulty, because the manual check shows the temperature is too high.

B: It can be faulty, I agree. We may check it again.

Exercise 3

*Read the following fax. Change the underlined phrases putting in an appropriate form of **may, might, can, could, must, mustn't** or **needn't**.*

```
date: 8 Nov        time: 12.47        from: 01273 548212
```

Further to our telephone conversation, <u>it is important that we</u> develop a superior organic fertiliser suitable for use by organic horticultural concerns and fruiterers. We <u>are in a position to</u> do this within six months. <u>It is not necessary to</u> greatly increase our research budget. In the short term, <u>it is possible that our Righton Research Laboratory will be able to</u> send us results of tests they carried out last year. In other words, <u>it is possible that we already have</u> the data we need.

In any case, <u>it is essential that we</u> develop this product as soon as possible. <u>It is important that we do not</u> let our competitors have this advantage.

I am away for a few days but <u>there is a chance that I will</u> call you on Monday.

UNIT 19

WILL, WOULD, MAY, MIGHT, CAN, COULD, MUST, MUSTN'T, NEEDN'T, SHALL, SHOULD (1)

See LOBE:
Unit 17 – **Will** and **would**
Unit 18 – **May** and **might**
Unit 19 – **Can** and **could**
Unit 20 – **Must, mustn't** and **needn't**
Unit 21 – **Shall** and **should**

Exercise 1

Match each of the pictures to the appropriate sentence below.

a

b

c

d

e

f

g

h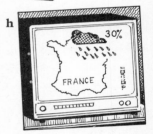

1　There may be rain tomorrow over northern France.
2　You needn't get a visa.
3　We must have an export licence.
4　I'll be arriving from Munich at 10 o'clock.
5　No-one should contaminate rivers.
6　Sales should continue to increase.
7　Only top management shall read the final report.
8　May I smoke?

Exercise 2

Read the following memo on purchasing procedure. Imagine you are reporting on the procedures in the memo. Say what happened, in the past tense. Begin: 'Authorisation for upgrading computer capability had to be obtained, if…'

Memorandum

From: Purchasing Department

To: Heads of Department

Authorisation for upgrading computer capability must be obtained, if the costs involved are more than $200. Staff can ask section supervisors for upgrades. Supervisors may ask for a written request. In this case, two people will together present the request. Later, they need to present a formal report on the application of the upgrade to the purchasing department.

WILL, WOULD, MAY, MIGHT, CAN, COULD, MUST, MUSTN'T, NEEDN'T, SHALL, SHOULD (2)

See LOBE:
Unit 17 – **Will** and **would**
Unit 18 – **May** and **might**
Unit 19 – **Can** and **could**
Unit 20 – **Must, mustn't** and **needn't**
Unit 21 – **Shall** and **should**

Exercise 1

Here is part of an item in the company newspaper for Honey Inc, a leisure products manufacturer. Complete the text by adding the right word from the box.

> can't must will will won't can
> might needn't should

Honey CD Rom
a complete information resource

We have developed a completely interactive CD-Rom package on Honey Inc. which _____ help all employees, customers and suppliers to know our company better. In fact, we _____ imagine anyone with links to Honey who _____ find the Honey CD Rom interesting and fun! With a simple-to-use format and a comprehensive Contents page, anyone _____ find the information they need. You _____ for example be interested in the history of the company, or its present exports partners, or research projects. You _____ find updated reports on every aspect of the company's activities, from staffing to sport and leisure opportunities, from new products to new development plans. Anyone connected with Honey _____ find plenty of interest. You _____ be an expert in computing, but you _____ have access to a computer, at home or at work.

The Honey CD Rom is available now, free! Send for your copy using the coupon on the back page.

Exercise 2

Look at the text from part of a leaflet enclosed with a hair and scalp treatment lotion, Dermox Gel. For each of the phrases below, make a sentence which includes a modal. The first is done as an example.

Dermox Gel

1 Hair and scalp treatment
2 Rub into the hair and scalp when dry.
3 Use a towel to protect the eyes during application.
4 Not to be used in combination with shampoos.
5 In some cases, irritation is possible.
6 If irritation occurs, see a doctor.
7 Do not swallow.
8 Dermox Gel is suitable for children over two years old.
9 Only one application is necessary.

Example:

1   *Dermox Gel **should** be used for hair and scalp treatment.*

UNIT 21

ACTIVE

See LOBE:
Unit 22 – Active

Exercise 1

The words in the following career history are jumbled up. Put them into the correct order.

1   a born David Packer in in Manchester near small town was 1948
2   where was the student school primary local he he average attended an
3   16 age and at business first he his left of school secondary started the
4   with when to supply success silicon signed Regents his he first deal chips came a
5   21st birthday by first had he his his made million
6   then shops selling retailing opened moved into hifi he five equipment and
7   a and assembled bought central components East Far from goods he in the
     the the workshop
8   years UK the than shops over more later he had five all 50
9   appliances decided diversify domestic he into other then to
10 when them sold shops ran outlets of many larger into his he he from competition

Exercise 2

Make 12 definitions by choosing the appropriate elements from the columns below.

1   A blue-collar worker is
2   A colleague is
3   A contract is
4   A director is
5   A grade is
6   A holiday is

7   A homeworker is
8   A job is
9   A moonlighter is
10 The personnel is
11 A superior is
12 A supervisor is

a company employee who	work for	several other (usually blue-collar) workers.
a legal agreement	within the structure	in a company.
a period of time	is in charge of	go to work.
someone who	of regular paid work	at home.
someone who	between	the same department or company or profession as you.
someone who	works	a manual job or in a job on the factory floor.
someone who	works in	a company.
someone who	works in	on it's Board of Directors.
someone who	when you do not have to	and another at night.
the level of a job	represents the shareholders of the company	of a company's workforce.
a position	has one job during the day	in the hierarchy of an organisation.
the total of all the people who	is above you	two people or parties.

ACTIVE and PASSIVE (1)

See LOBE:
Unit 22 – Active
Unit 23 – Passive

Exercise 1

Form passive sentences from the following active sentences. Some can be put into more than one passive sentence.

1 The bank sends us a bank statement every month.
2 We study the statement very carefully.
3 We inform them of any mistakes.
4 The bank contacts us regularly to review our business.
5 This is likely to cause us some problems.

Exercise 2

*Suggest a passive sentence for the following signs, saying what **can be, can't be, must be** or **mustn't be** done.*

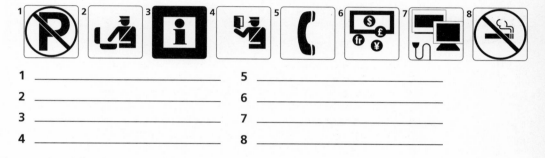

1 _____   5 _____

2 _____   6 _____

3 _____   7 _____

4 _____   8 _____

Exercise 3

Put the following active sentences into the passive, making any other changes to improve the style of your final sentences.

1   This transparency shows the manufacture of boards.

   _____

2   We have always bought the rods from local suppliers.

   _____

3   Who checks the quality of the raw materials?

   _____

4   That machine there is cutting the rods into boards.

   _____

5   After that we must insert the components into the boards.

   _____

6   Last year we had to install a faster drilling machine.

   _____

7.   We should see the benefits of faster production next year.

   _____

8   In five years we are going to introduce a completely new process.

   _____

UNIT 23

ACTIVE and PASSIVE (2)

See LOBE:
Unit 22 – Active
Unit 23 – Passive

Exercise 1

Choose the best clause to complete the following sentences.

1	Although this book was written some years ago,	**a**	it must have been withdrawn.
2	Because this book is inaccurate,	**b**	it should have been withdrawn years ago.
3	If it had been my decision,	**c**	it can't have been withdrawn.
4	If you can't find the book in any bookshop,	**d**	it might only have been withdrawn from some bookshops.
5	If you can find the book in London,	**e**	it needn't have been withdrawn from the shops.
6	I'm sure I saw a copy of the book, so	**f**	it would have been withdrawn years ago.

Exercise 2

*Complete the responses to the following statements explaining what **must have been/should have been/might have been/needn't have been/would have been/could have been** done in the following situations, using the verb in brackets. The first one has been done for you.*

1 *We haven't received an acknowledgement for our order yet.*
   I apologise. The order _____ (acknowledge) by 30 June.
   I apologise. The order should have been acknowledged by 30 June.
2 *We haven't received an invoice yet.*
   I'm sorry. You _____ (invoice) at the end of the month.
3 *We couldn't lease the company cars last year.*
   But the regulations have changed and _____ (lease) this year.
4 *I have checked this bill and we have definitely paid too much.*
   Yes, there's been a mistake and you _____ (over-charge).
5 *We thought we had to pay in advance.*
   Not at all, the bill _____ (pay) in advance.
6 *We paid the invoice by credit card.*
   You should have seen in our payment conditions that it _____ (pay) by cheque.
7 *I can't find any record of your order.*
   So do you think the order _____ (cancel)?
8 *I don't understand why we have received this delivery.*
   It's very simple. An order _____ (place) by someone in your organisation.
9 *We didn't receive the discount you offered.*
   To receive the discount, the goods _____ (re-order) within 30 days.

Exercise 3

Rewrite the following sentences from a legal report. Start each sentence with the underlined word(s) and make any other necessary changes. The first one has been done for you.

1 We believe <u>the defendant</u> entered the house by climbing in through a window.
   The defendant is believed to have entered the house by climbing in through a window.
2 We think he brought an accomplice with him.
   _____
3 We don't believe <u>the accomplice</u> entered the house.
   _____
4 The owners reported that <u>many items of jewellery</u> had been stolen.
   _____
5 However, we feel that <u>the owners</u> helped the burglar.
   _____
6 We know that <u>the owners</u> made an exaggerated insurance claim.
   _____
7 We understand that <u>the owners</u> left the country last week.
   _____
8 We don't expect that <u>they</u> will return until the defendant is behind bars.
   _____

See LOBE:
Unit 24 – **Be** (1)
Unit 25 – **Be** (2)

Exercise 1

Are the following sentences right or wrong? If wrong, correct them.

1 How are you keeping?
2 I guess I'm just lucky, aren't I?
3 The situation always is difficult at this time of year.
4 Why are you being so pessimistic? Don't be.
5 It's still time to change the forecast for next year.
6 The prototype has been being under construction for the last six months.

Exercise 2

Complete the following quotations with an appropriate form of the verb **to be,** *and* **it** *or* **there,** *where necessary.*

1 *Business? _____ quite simple: _____ other people's money.*

(Alexandre Dumas, 1824–95, French dramatist)

2 *_____ good in business _____ the most fascinating kind of art ....*

Making money _____ art and working _____ art and good

business _____ the best art.

(Andy Warhol, 1928–87, US pop artist)

3 *Deals _____ my art form.*

(Donald Trump, b. 1946, US businessman)

4 *Having money _____ rather like _____ a blonde.*

_____ more fun but not vital.

(Mary Quant, b. 1936, British fashion designer)

Exercise 3

Complete the following extract from a newspaper article with an appropriate form of the verb **to be,** *and* **it** *or* **there,** *where necessary.*

_____ few people with the same charisma as Halmet Entacre. Born into a large rural family in Southern Rotaronga, _____ many occasions when the family _____ without food. Halmet soon decided that country life _____ not for him and often said, 'One day I _____ rich and famous.' But _____ not until the Second World War that _____ an opportunity to move to the capital. While he _____ working in a factory producing weapons, he _____ noticed by the owner. He _____ soon promoted to the position of factory manager. When the war ended he started his first business exporting clothes to the West. With the West desperate to rebuild economies, _____ relatively easy to find markets for his goods. His clothing empire _____ at the forefront of the Rotarongan economy for more than 40 years now. In a recent interview, Halmet said that most of his ambitions _____ fulfilled. 'Without _____ immodest, _____ no doubt I have come a long way from my village.'

UNIT 25

VERBS OF SPEAKING: SAY, TELL, TALK, SPEAK and DISCUSS

See LOBE:
Unit 26 – Verbs of speaking

Exercise 1

Are the following sentences right or wrong? If wrong, correct them.

1 Can I speak with Ivan Tyler, please?
2 Mr Tyler has just said that he can't speak to you now.
3 But he told me to call him today at 11 o'clock.
4 He discussed with me last week about the need for a new supplier.
5 He told that they were dissatisfied with their present supplier.
6 Can you say him that I'll call back later.
7 I've just talked to him and he'd like you to call tomorrow.

Exercise 2

*Complete the interview with Bengt Stockman, the CEO of Magnus Electronics, by using one of the following verbs in the correct tense: **say, tell, talk, speak** or **discuss**.*

Interviewer: What _____ you _____ to your competitors who _____ of your lack of environmental concern?

Bengt: Firstly, they should _____ to the various environmental groups I support. And, secondly, they should _____ our record with the relevant governmental department.

Interviewer: And what will they _____ ?

Bengt: Basically, they _____ that I have always observed all the rules and regulations.

Interviewer: But that's not what your former Managing Director _____ . In a recent report he _____ of the toxic emissions from your factories.

Bengt: Please _____ him to provide us with some proof. There's not a shred of evidence of any improper practices. My position is clear. As I _____ on many occasions, we have nothing to hide. And I am happy to _____ our environmental record with the highest authorities.

Interviewer: Is it true that you _____ a reporter from the Green Lobby that you had no time for ecologists?

Bengt: Yes, but I _____ it in the context of a lot of untrue statements made in the press about my activities.

Interviewer: So, you don't deny _____ that.

Bengt: No, absolutely not.

Exercise 3

*Complete the following common phrases with an appropriate verb: **say, tell, talk, speak** or **discuss**.*

1 As I _____ before, ...
2 When we _____ about this matter last week, ...
3 As I _____ you before, ...
4 Last week they _____ that ...
5 When we _____ this matter last week, ...
6 I'd like to _____ to you again about this matter, because ...
7 We can _____ them to ...

Exercise 1

Match the following verbs of reporting on the left with their meaning on the right.

1	to agree	**a**	to argue forcefully
2	to deny	**b**	to win someone over by reason or advice
3	to promise	**c**	to commit oneself to do or give
4	to declare	**d**	to come to an understanding
5	to refuse	**e**	to make aware in advance of harm or danger
6	to urge	**f**	not to agree
7	to suggest	**g**	to say that something is not true
8	to warn	**h**	to request formally
9	to persuade	**i**	to propose
10	to invite	**j**	to state authoritatively

Exercise 2

*Replace the verb **say** in the following sentences with one of the above verbs of reporting with a similar meaning. Use each verb once and make any necessary change.*

1 The Finance Director said with authority that the cashflow situation was very serious.
2 He said that there would be problems if they didn't reduce overheads.
3 They said that there had not been any unnecessary expenditure.
4 He said that they were welcome to review his proposals.
5 He said forcefully that they must take appropriate action.
6 He said that he would review the figures before the next meeting.
7 He said convincingly that he was of the same opinion as the MD that they should investigate the costs of outsourcing.
8 He said that it was only reasonable that they should join the company in finding a solution.
9 He said that his proposal was to reduce the workforce.
10 They said that they were not willing to accept his suggestions.

Exercise 3

Complete the following extract from a letter with an appropriate verb from the box.

estimate   invite   inform   notify
believe   agree   guarantee   urge

```
Dear investor

We would like to ──────── you to take part in
the investment opportunity of the year. In fact we
──────── you not to miss this unique chance to
make your money work for you. We ──────── that
this is a once-in-a-lifetime investment. If you
──────── to set aside a small sum every month
for the next five years, we ──────── a staggering
105 per cent interest at the end of the period. We
──────── that this return will far outstrip the
rate of inflation during the period.

If you would like to participate, please
──────── us by phone or ──────── us using
the reply coupon.
```

UNIT 27

BE, HAVE, HAVE GOT, GET, MAKE and DO

See LOBE:
Unit 24 – **Be** (1)
Unit 25 – **Be** (2)
Unit 31 – **Have, have got** and **get**
Unit 32 – **Make** versus **do**

Exercise 1

Two colleagues are discussing their Rotarongan subsidiary. Complete the following dialogue with an appropriate form of one of the verbs from the box.

be	have	have got	get	make	do

Michael: So how _____ your trip to Rotaronga?

Jenny: In fact we _____ a very interesting time. Our subsidiary is _____ very good business at present.

Michael: How many people _____ they _____ working for them now?

Jenny: They've just _____ a recruitment drive and now there _____ exactly 32 people.

Michael: And what impression did you _____ of the new management?

Jenny: I must say I was very impressed. They certainly _____ commitment. I think they'll _____ a great success of it.

Michael: I'm glad to hear that you _____ such optimism!

Jenny: Well, yes! I'm sure they're _____ all the right things and will _____ it work.

Exercise 2

*A late delivery to a customer may have serious consequences for this company. Complete the following memo to the warehouse manager with an appropriate form of **have, have got** or **get** and make any necessary changes in word order.*

Memorandum _____

To: PG
From: NS

We _____ a letter from our solicitor this morning. He says that he _____ the report about the claim but he _____ problems arranging a meeting to discuss the terms. Our customers are claiming that the delivery _____ to France four weeks late. By that time they _____ not _____ any chance to complete the project on time, so they _____ in touch with their lawyers to cancel the shipment. Unfortunately, our solicitor _____ not _____ their

Exercise 3

*Use **make** or **do** to form 12 business phrases.*

1 We _____ a good profit from our exports.
2 We _____ business all over the world.
3 We intend to _____ an effort to reach new markets next year.
4 What did you _____ at university?
5 We will _____ the last payment next week.
6 We're not here to _____ a loss!
7 The bookkeeper will _____ the books after his holidays.
8 It used to be easier to _____ money.
9 I've got to _____ some work at the office this evening.
10 I hope to _____ an agreement with a local supplier.
11 I'm sure we can _____ well.
12 What do you _____ for a living?

See LOBE:
Unit 28 – Verbs of the senses
Unit 30 – Verbs + adjectives
Unit 33 – Verb + preposition
Unit 34 – Verb + object + preposition
Unit 35 – Verb + adverb

Exercise 1

Circle the 'odd man out' in the following groups.

1 look	sound	feel	taste	eat	smell
2 look	sound	watch	see	look at	appear
3 look after	look at	look for	look forward to	look like	look up
4 look	allow	apply	hope	sound	apologise
5 prohibit	allow	prevent	stop	forbid	ban
6 look up	call off	go up	speak up	speed up	turn up

Exercise 2

A wine-producing company is reviewing its yearly sales. Complete the following extract from its presentation with appropriate forms of verbs of the senses.

If you _____ the transparency, you'll _____ that turnover has increased by 12 per cent over the last year. At first, this rise _____ very encouraging for our medium-term strategy; however, this result masks the area of overheads, which, I _____ , have grown by a disproportionate amount. This is an area which we really must _____ . Later today we will _____ from Paul Brown, who will discuss ways of controlling costs.

Now let's _____ the results in some specific areas. The new wine range has been well received. The verdict on the Rotarongan Chardonnay is that it _____ very fresh with just the right bouquet of fruit blossom, although some judges said it _____ a little dry. The unanimous conclusion on appearance was that it has a nice colour and _____ good in the new-style bottle. The judges were less complimentary about the advertising jingle, which they said _____ rather childish. We'll _____ it again later.

Exercise 3

Mr Zezuli is visiting a textile manufacturer. Complete the following mini-dialogues with appropriate prepositions or adverbs.

Extract 1 The Sales Manager is just preparing herself for her visitor and asks her Personal Assistant to talk to him for a few minutes.
SM: Anna, do you think you could look _____ Mr Zezuli for a few minutes? I'll be right with him.
PA: Mr Zezuli, while you're waiting perhaps you'd like to look _____ our latest fabrics.
Z: Can I look _____ the catalogues? I'd like to see your whole product range first.

Extract 2 The Sales Manager is with Mr Zezuli.
SM: Mr Zezuli, if you'd like to look _____ , we can arrange a visit to the factory. So, first I suggest that we look _____ the plant. Now, if you look _____ _____ the window, you'll see a convoy of lorries leaving the depot.

Extract 3 The Sales Manager and Mr Zezuli are walking to the factory.
SM: In this corridor, you can see paintings of the directors. This is the present MD. I've always looked _____ _____ her, because I think she manages the company efficiently.

Extract 4 The Sales Manager and Mr Zezuli are discussing prices.
A: I'm afraid I'm not happy with these figures. We should look _____ them in more detail.
SM: So, I hope you'll find these more acceptable.
Z: Yes, I do. So, now let's look _____ to my next visit and make some provisional plans.
SM: Yes, Mr Zezuli, I look _____ _____ meeting you on your next visit to Rotaronga. Let's…

UNIT ◆29◆
VERB PATTERNS (2)

See LOBE:
Unit 28 – Verbs of the senses
Unit 30 – Verbs + adjectives
Unit 33 – Verb + preposition
Unit 34 – Verb + object + preposition
Unit 35 – Verb + adverb

Exercise 1

Circle the 'odd man out' in the following groups.

1 become	fall	turn	remain	get	grow
2 allow	authorise	stop	help	permit	enable
3 amount	conform	refer	consent	forget	belong
4 comment	succeed	depend	rely	focus	concentrate

Exercise 2

Complete the following memo by selecting an appropriate verb from the list below and adding the correct preposition.

compare   prevent   welcome   exclude   help   provide
divide   spend   describe   inform   replace   limit

memo

This memo is to _____ all members of the steering committee
_____ the details of the next international meeting. I
shall _____ you _____ a list of tasks that need to be
done. We will _____ a little time _____ finalising the
schedule at our next internal meeting. Unfortunately, my trip to
Japan will _____ me _____ taking part in the meeting.
I think we should _____ the programme for the day
_____ three parts.

The first session is to _____ our foreign guests _____
the company and to _____ our operations _____ them. As
time is short, we will need to _____ this part _____
the essentials – of course without _____ any key personnel
_____ the proceedings.

In the second part of the programme, we should _____ our
working practices _____ those in other companies. We have
already made it clear that we intend to _____ some
practices _____ more modern ones and this could be a
fruitful area for discussion.

Finally, we will _____ the participants _____ the more
complex norms which need...

Exercise 3

Complete the following sentences with appropriate prepositions or adverbs.

1   Could you put me _____ _____ Helmut Brinkmayer, please?

2   Good morning, Mr Brinkmayer. As we are ready to proceed, I'd like to bring _____
    the date of our next meeting.

3   We're facing some problems here. Would it be possible to put delivery _____ till
    next month?

4   We're looking for someone to put some money _____ the business.

5   If we can't find some extra capital, we'll have to put the business _____ for sale.

6   I find it very difficult to put _____ _____ this uncertainty.

7   We need to make a decision today. We can't put it _____ any longer.

See LOBE:
Unit 28 – Verbs of the senses
Unit 30 – Verbs + adjectives
Unit 33 – Verb + preposition
Unit 34 – Verb + object + preposition
Unit 35 – Verb + adverb

Exercise 1

Are the following sentences right or wrong? If wrong, correct them.

1 I'm feeling very well, thanks.
2 Don't worry if you can't find the letter now. You can look after it later.
3 Did you look at that programme on the TV last night?
4 Petrol prices have remained steady since the early '90s.
5 I'll pick up you at your hotel at 7 o'clock, if that suits you.
6 We can discuss about the proposals over dinner.
7 I'll ask to my secretary to fax you the documents this afternoon.
8 The new investment will permit us to improve the plant.

Exercise 2

Two old colleagues meet each other at a conference. Replace the underlined verbs in the dialogue with a phrasal verb from the box below.

turn down	fill in	take on	put forward	turn out
get away from	come across	give up	stand for	get on

Bill: Nigel! How are you <u>doing</u>?
Nigel: Fine, thanks, Bill.
Bill: I hear you recently <u>stopped</u> working for Alpha.
Nigel: Yes, they <u>rejected</u> my application for the post of Marketing Manager.
Bill: So did they <u>employ</u> someone from outside?
Nigel: Yes, though in the end I was glad to <u>leave</u> Alpha. It <u>proved</u> to be a good move.
Bill: Really!
Nigel: While I was deciding what to do, I <u>met</u> an old friend from university. And he <u>proposed</u> a number of very interesting work ideas. And in the end I <u>completed</u> an ad in the paper for a franchise, called CLSS.
Bill: And what does that abbreviation <u>mean</u>?
Nigel: Criminal Lawyer Support Services.

Exercise 3

Complete the following sentences with appropriate particles (prepositions or adverbs).

1 We tried to find a replacement for Fred, but finally we decided to take him _____ .

2 Why don't you take _____ that old sign? It looks terrible.

3 It's recruitment time. We are taking _____ a number of new junior managers at the moment.

4 That product is a real success; it has taken _____ in a big way.

5 We are conducting a survey. It won't take _____ more than a few minutes of your time.

6 We expect that BusCom will try to take us _____ in the near future.

UNIT 31

SENTENCE TYPES

See LOBE:
Unit 36 – Sentence types – simple and complex

Exercise 1

Look at the advertisement for a pension scheme. Classify the sentence types of sentences 1–12 according to patterns in the table below.

	Simple sentence	Complex sentence connected by		
		coordination	subordination	general purpose connector
Statement				
Question				
Command				
Exclamation				

1	Would you like to retire in comfort?
2	Have you thought about how much money you'll need to retire in comfort?
3	If the answer is yes, then the retirement bond could be for you.
4	For a small monthly payment, we will ensure that you enjoy your retirement years.
5	How do you subscribe?
6	This is a strictly limited offer which we know will soon be fully subscribed.
7	Act quickly to avoid disappointment.
8	You can buy your bond through your financial advisor or we will be happy to arrange it for you.
9	In either case you need to act quickly.
10	Buy a retirement bond and enjoy your retirement!
11	What an easy step to take!
12	Don't delay.

Exercise 2

Write a letter based on the following draft. Use as many different sentence types as possible.

```
Dear investor
Growth or income?
If answer both, bonus bond ideal investment for you.
Bonus bond:
  1. growth - expect 2 per cent per year, based performance UK stock market
  2. income - guaranteed 2 per cent per year
Investment limits?
Minimum investment £10,000; maximum £100,000
How to subscribe?
Easy. Just complete application form enclosed with letter; send it with
cheque in the envelope provided.
Remember act quickly - offer closes soon.
More information, call financial advisor; or our offices.
```

Exercise 1

Find 11 adverbial connectors in the following word box.

H	I	O	P	L	K	B	V	T	Y	U	I	F
G	G	Y	J	U	Y	N	L	Y	P	A	O	I
L	U	Q	Q	P	U	A	K	J	O	S	I	N
O	W	P	P	T	O	C	T	S	L	H	Y	A
P	R	N	O	H	P	T	U	I	I	O	H	L
L	I	A	E	E	M	U	B	M	U	W	N	L
A	L	T	E	R	N	A	T	I	V	E	L	Y
S	G	U	Y	E	W	L	A	L	L	V	M	P
T	J	R	R	F	A	L	E	A	K	E	B	O
L	L	A	B	O	S	Y	R	R	H	R	V	L
Y	O	L	N	R	D	E	Y	L	T	D	C	K
E	P	L	M	E	F	A	N	Y	W	A	Y	J
U	Q	Y	A	W	G	L	I	A	R	F	X	M
P	T	U	R	I	N	S	T	E	A	D	A	N
Q	J	I	T	P	H	O	C	E	E	H	S	V

Exercise 2

Complete the following advertisement with an appropriate linking word or phrase from the list below.

> naturally   that is to say   then   also   in other words   after that   but
> then   so   yet   as well as   obviously   however   to start with

---

ADVENTURE HOLIDAYS FOR MANAGERS

If you need a challenge, _____ our **ADVENTURE HOLIDAYS** could be the answer.

Our weekend programmes provide opportunities for developing leadership qualities within a tough _____ supportive group environment. _____, we'll sharpen you up as an individual _____ making you into a top-class team player.

The weekend is spent at our training centre in the beautiful Lake District. _____, you'll want some comfort, _____ we've taken over a small castle, but _____ you'll have to get past the guards. We start on a Friday evening without dinner. _____ there is an orientation session. _____ it's down to business. You'll spend most of your weekend outside, working with others on a variety of intellectually and physically challenging activities. _____ there's a warm bed waiting for you after you've finished the course.

You can expect to return home on Sunday evening a changed person, _____ ready to face any new challenges.

_____, we hope you'll _____ return for another **ADVENTURE WEEKEND** at some future date. _____, most of our graduates find that they don't need to.

For more information, contact **Mike Barker** on

0171-556-8967 (phone) or *0171-457-0553* (fax)

UNIT 33

LINKING IDEAS (2)

See LOBE:
Unit 38 – Subordinate clauses
Units 42–47 – Subordinate clauses

Exercise 1

Each of the following sentences contains a mistake. Identify the mistakes and correct them.

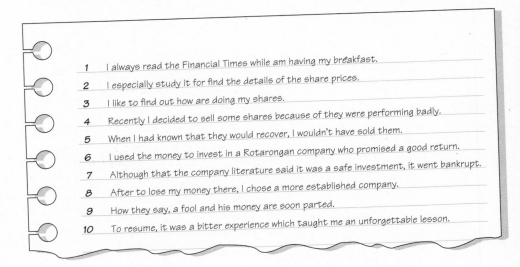

1 I always read the Financial Times while am having my breakfast.
2 I especially study it for find the details of the share prices.
3 I like to find out how are doing my shares.
4 Recently I decided to sell some shares because of they were performing badly.
5 When I had known that they would recover, I wouldn't have sold them.
6 I used the money to invest in a Rotarongan company who promised a good return.
7 Although that the company literature said it was a safe investment, it went bankrupt.
8 After to lose my money there, I chose a more established company.
9 How they say, a fool and his money are soon parted.
10 To resume, it was a bitter experience which taught me an unforgettable lesson.

Exercise 2

Underline the subordinate clauses in the following sentences and then classify them in the table below.

1 While customs are different around the world, good manners are appreciated everywhere.
2 Kordab Bronsaw is a Rotarongan sociologist who has studied various societies.
3 On the subject of Rotaronga, he has said that local habits are very easy to follow.
4 Rotarongans have had a lot of contact with foreigners, so they understand different cultures.
5 Kordab has written a short guide so that visitors to the country will know how to behave.
6 If you are invited for dinner, come on time.
7 Guests should bring a small gift when they are invited to a person's house.
8 Because Rotarongans are very hospitable, your glass and plate will always be full.
9 Your hosts will be inquisitive and will want to know what you think of their country.

Reported question	Condition	Time	Relative clause	Contrast	Purpose	Reported speech	Cause	Result

Exercise 3

Combine a clause on the left with one on the right to make six meaningful sentences.

1	We studied the share price	**a**	because their value is rising.
2	We bought shares	**b**	so that we would know the best time to buy.
3	We will keep the shares	**c**	until the market becomes less volatile.
4	We will sell the shares	**d**	if their value increases by 50 per cent.
5	The trader said	**e**	when the price was right.
6	We won't invest in any more shares	**f**	that now was a good time to sell.

See LOBE:
Unit 38 – Subordinate clauses
Units 42–47 – Subordinate clauses

Exercise 1

Circle the 'odd man out' in the following groups.

1	though	because	whereas	although	while
2	who	which	when	what	where
3	for to	so that	in order that	so as to	in order to
4	after	before	until	if	as soon as
5	if	whereas	provided that	in case	unless

Exercise 2

Combine the following pairs of sentences about ABC using the subordinating marker shown.

1 ABC is a small engineering company. It makes pumps. (-ing clause)

2 The recession hit the building industry. At the same time we saw our orders declining. (when)

3 We cut back on the workforce. However, this was not enough to protect our position. (although)

4 We saw the benefits of introducing a quality system. Then we started a project to investigate the advantages ourselves. (after)

5 We needed to improve quality. That's why we asked the production line workers to contribute suggestions. (because)

6 We set up a number of quality circles. The purpose was to find out how the quality of our manufacturing processes could be improved. (in order to)

7 Some of the workers' ideas were accepted. But others were rejected. (whereas)

8 Quality improved. Immediately we saw an increase in our customers. (as soon as)

9 We have consolidated our position. Now we are ready to expand again. (-ing clause)

Exercise 3

Complete the following letter by writing in the missing subordinating conjunctions.

Dear Mr Jackson

—————— living and working in London has become more expensive and less pleasant and —————— we need to expand, we have decided to move our operations to York next year. —————— York will not offer the range of facilities of the capital, we are sure that it will provide the right working environment —————— the company can thrive. —————— maintain contact with our customers, we have been building up a database and would be grateful —————— you could check that your details are correct. Please be sure to return the form to us in the envelope provided —————— we can update our records and keep you informed. —————— we move, we intend to pass on the savings to our valued clients and —————— we are installed we shall be writing to you again telling you of our exciting new developments.

Yours sincerely

Alan Baker

Alan Baker
Public Relations

UNIT 35

REPORTED SPEECH (1)

See LOBE:
Unit 27 – Verbs of reporting
Unit 39 – Reported speech (1)
Unit 40 – Reported speech (2)

Exercise 1

Find 14 verbs of reporting in the following word box.

S	A	F	H	I	L	U	B	N	D	W	E
R	T	D	E	S	C	R	I	B	E	E	T
G	U	I	O	P	K	G	E	T	C	R	I
A	S	A	G	R	E	E	T	Y	L	K	D
C	B	N	I	O	P	L	K	J	I	E	E
C	O	N	F	I	R	M	A	S	N	D	C
Q	U	O	T	H	J	I	K	T	E	L	L
C	S	U	G	G	E	S	T	L	O	P	A
C	U	N	A	S	D	F	O	I	W	P	R
B	A	C	P	G	O	L	S	T	A	T	E
E	R	E	F	U	S	E	H	I	R	E	T
A	C	D	E	E	F	K	I	L	N	T	I
G	O	I	L	S	N	I	M	R	T	E	Y
A	D	V	I	S	E	A	F	R	A	H	Y

Exercise 2

Put the following headlines into reported speech using a suitable verb of reporting in the past tense.

1 Marketing Director

Let's introduce the new measures immediately.

Have you calculated the final figures?

2 Finance Director

Be careful with recruitment.

3 Personnel Manager

I'll review the situation next week.

4 Managing Director

5 Production Manager

I am going to resign.

I'll sell the patents if I don't get my extra budget!

6 R & D Manager

The company should appoint a new management team.

7 Chairman of the Board

See LOBE:
Unit 27 – Verbs of reporting
Unit 39 – Reported speech (1)
Unit 40 – Reported speech (2)

Exercise 1

Are the following sentences right or wrong? If wrong, then correct them.

1 In the meeting we advised to invest more money in research.
2 We told them that the present lab needed extending.
3 They asked how much money did we need.
4 We explained how we reached the final total.
5 They agreed looking at the figures again.
6 We said that we would meet again the following week.
7 He asked us to don't reveal the figures to anyone else.
8 We replied that we would keep them confidential.

Exercise 2

Here is an extract from a meeting in which a company's financial problems are being discussed. Complete the report of the meeting.

John: We face a serious problem and need to cut the company's running costs by at least 12 per cent. If we don't, then we may face closure.
Mary: So, why don't we look for areas where savings can be made?
Alan: I can't agree with the proposed budget cut. In fact, if my department's budget is reduced, it will be very difficult for us to meet the targets.
John: Yes, but please remember that if we can't make the savings, then there will be no targets to meet.
Alan: But if my budget is cut, then there will be no products to sell. Unless we have the new products for the beginning of next year, we'll lose many of our customers. Then we'll be in the same position as we were when we started 10 years ago.
John: I realise that we face a serious problem, but we need to find a workable solution.

John pointed out that the company _____ .

He warned that _____ .

Mary suggested _____ .

Alan stated that _____ .

He warned that _____ .

John reminded him that _____ .

Alan replied that _____ . *He added that*

_____ *and that then they*

would be in the same position they were _____ .

John answered that _____ , *but emphasised*

that _____ .

Exercise 3

Put the sentences from the report of an interview into the correct order. The first one has been done for you.

He agreed to discuss this with the rest of the team and let me know the following week. ( )
I warned that any delay could mean that our competitors might overtake us. ( )
He reassured me that there was little chance of that. ( )
I asked when the new prototype would be introduced. (1)
He replied that they were still testing it, but hoped to have it ready by the summer. ( )
I proposed that we fix a date for the presentation of the prototype. ( )

UNIT 37
QUESTIONS (1)

See LOBE:
Unit 39 – Reported speech (1)
Unit 40 – Reported speech (2)
Unit 41 – Questions
Unit 90 – Requesting information and action

Exercise 1

What is the **wh**-question word/phrase if you want to find out about:

1 people _____
2 things _____
3 time _____
4 place _____
5 reason _____
6 manner _____
7 length of time _____
8 distance _____
9 quantity and amount _____
10 dimensions _____

Exercise 2

Are the following questions right or wrong? If wrong, correct them.

1 Where are you born?
2 What do you do?
3 When did you joined your present company?
4 How long time have you worked in that department?
5 Why you changed your job?
6 What is happen to the payment?
7 I'd like to know if the payment did arrive yesterday.
8 I'm afraid I don't know about what payment you are talking.
9 Why you didn't inform us earlier abut this error?
10 If do you have any questions, I'll be happy to answer them.

Exercise 3

A journalist is interviewing Paul Johnson, the famous industrialist. What are the journalist's questions? Complete the following interview by writing the questions.

J: Paul Johnson, you've lived here for many years. But you're not from this country, are you?
_____ ?

P: In fact I was born in a small village in Rotaronga.

J: _____ ?

P: I left when I was 15 years old.

J: _____ ?

P: I decided to leave because there were very few opportunities.

J: _____ ?

P: First I went to the capital.

J: _____ ?

P: About five years.

J: And then you came here. _____ ?

P: I've lived here since the early '80s.

J: _____ ?

P: Yes, it was very difficult to make a start here.

J: In fact you have built up a very successful retailing business. _____ ?

P: At the moment we are working on a diversification plan. But at present it's secret.

J: You are one of the biggest employers in your sector. _____ ?

P: We employ about 30,000 people.

J: You are a prolific traveller. _____ ?

P: About 250,000 miles each year, I think.

J: _____ ?

P: I plan to continue this intensive lifestyle for another few years.

J: _____ ?

P: My main ambition is to return to my country and retire there.

See LOBE:
Unit 39 – Reported speech (1)
Unit 40 – Reported speech (2)
Unit 41 – Questions
Unit 90 – Requesting information and action

Exercise 1

Rearrange the words in the following sentences to make 10 questions (direct or indirect).

1 any contacts did during make trip useful you your?
2 your you which visit to see New York during did consultants?
3 foreign from our spoke subsidiary to who you?
4 writing when we to their receive order in going are?
5 do extra from get manage orders the think to we where will you?
6 wait us to to they long like know I'd how expect.
7 cost how much package the total us will?
8 you will to the people need many install how equipment?
9 current far got have how on project the we?
10 you you why were us the problems inform facing earlier didn't about?

Exercise 2

Rearrange the following sentences to make a telephone conversation. The first one has been done for you.

A: Could I speak to John Fowler, please? (1)
A: Elena Bronowski. ( )
A: I'd like to find out if he can arrange some advertising for us. ( )
A: OK, but could you give me Mr Fowler's direct number? ( )
A: My name is Elena Bronowski.( )
A: Sorry, what did you say? ( )
A: Yes, certainly. It's B ( )
A: Yes, R-O-N-O-W-S-K-I. ( )
B: Yes, it's 437-0028. ( )
B: And what's it in connection with? ( )
B: I'm sorry, he's in a meeting. D'you think you could call back later? ( )
B: And your name again was …? ( )
B : For Berlin? ( )
B: I'm sorry. Could you spell that for me, please? ( )
B: I asked why you wanted to speak to John Fowler. ( )
B: Just hold on, please, Mrs Bronowski… ( )
B: Who's speaking, please? ( )

Exercise 3

Rewrite the following direct questions as indirect questions, using the polite formula shown.

1 How long have you known Vassili Theodopoulos? (please tell us)
2 Where did you last see him? (we would like to know)
3 Did you suspect anything about his company's operations? (we would like to ask you)
4 Why didn't you contact us sooner about your suspicions? (the police would like to know)
5 Who contacted you after your last meeting with him? (could you tell us)
6 When are you going to Greece next? (do you think you could tell us)
7 Will you be visiting his offices in Athens? (I wonder if you'd mind telling us)
8 Have you ever been involved in any illegal activities? (I was wondering if we could ask you)

See LOBE:
Unit 48 – Nouns
Unit 49 – Noun compounds

Exercise 1

Find seven pairs of countable and uncountable nouns with connected meanings in the following word box.

A	C	C	O	M	M	O	D	A	T	I	O	N	S
D	W	A	E	R	T	Y	I	O	L	P	T	K	D
V	B	S	U	G	G	E	S	T	I	O	N	M	E
I	A	E	G	H	L	Q	N	M	Y	T	R	E	V
C	S	T	R	E	L	U	G	G	A	G	E	L	I
E	C	R	I	T	E	I	F	L	I	G	R	E	C
S	T	R	T	R	I	P	P	E	T	A	B	L	E
A	R	O	U	M	E	M	E	E	R	P	A	O	L
F	A	S	H	O	T	E	L	T	A	Y	O	R	L
C	F	T	O	P	M	N	T	R	V	A	R	R	S
D	F	U	R	N	I	T	U	R	E	A	T	Y	R
B	I	G	H	D	E	T	H	Y	L	I	A	N	B
S	C	V	U	I	L	M	N	Q	U	E	R	T	G

Exercise 2

Circle the correct form in the following letter.

In this bulletin I would like to give you the most recent information/informations about the company's finances. Since the acquisition by Megacorp our asset/assets has/have risen by 65 per cent and our debt/debts has/have fallen by 25 per cent. Megacorp have provided us with additional fund/funds which we can use to develop the business and have given us permission/permissions to use this money as we see fit. The financial restructuring has involved a lot of work/works and travel/travels and I should like to extend thank/thanks to the whole management team who have been so supportive during this difficult period. The future of the company is now secured and we will be looking to moving our headquarter/headquarters to York in the near future. This will enable us to release some of our capital/capitals and reduce our liability/liabilities.

Exercise 3

Match the phrases on the left (1–10) with appropriate phrases on the right (a–j) to make 10 sentences.

1	The information	a	coming out of Rotaronga is quite depressing.
2	The people	b	are located just outside New York.
3	The equipment	c	you requested is in the post.
4	Travel	d	she gave us was to sell out immediately.
5	The news	e	we are going to move to are ideal.
6	The advice	f	we want to reach are all in this area.
7	Their headquarters	g	we offered was not enough for them.
8	The premises	h	we are going to employ will work in the field.
9	The money	i	we bought from you is not functioning properly.
10	The personnel	j	broadens the mind.

Exercise 1

Form a noun compound from the following phrases.

1 the management of assets
2 a claim for insurance
3 a sheet which shows the balance of a company
4 a man who is responsible for sales
5 a subsidiary which is overseas
6 a subsidy from the government
7 a person who holds shares
8 a person/company holding the majority of the shares
9 a car which belongs to the company
10 a study of the techniques of production
11 a report of progress for management
12 a manufacturer of components for computers

Exercise 2

Label the departments in the following plan with noun compounds based on the information given.

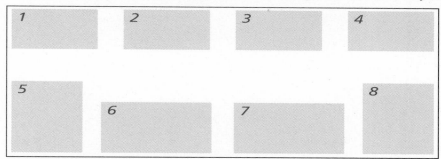

1 the department which carries out research into the market
2 the department which looks after relations with employees
3 the department which carries out research into new products
4 the department which is responsible for the welfare of employees
5 the department which provides a service of processing data
6 the department which is responsible for the drafting of contracts
7 the department which is responsible for the control of quality
8 the department which handles relations with customers

Exercise 3

Rewrite the following text using as many noun compounds as possible.

The producers of paper are celebrating prices and profits which are a record. Groups in the industry of forestry have surprised analysts in the city with bumper earnings. One producer of newsprint has moved from loss to profit in one year. Of course, increases in prices have helped and further rises of price are in the pipeline. The buoyancy of the market for paper is reflected in hikes in prices for paper for laser printers and photocopiers. Measures for the cutting of costs in the industry have also led to better figures. But producers are worried about measures for the conservation of paper which could have an impact on consumption.

UNIT 41
NOUNS (3)

See LOBE:
Unit 48 – Nouns
Unit 49 – Noun compounds

Exercise 1

Label the following extract from a balance sheet by selecting the correct term from the pairs given in the box below, which correspond to the phrases in brackets on the balance sheet.

Microcorp

_____	as at 31 December 19 ___	(statement of company's position at a certain date)
_____	£000	(things belonging to the company)
_____		(property/equipment owned by the company)
_____	340	(ground)
_____	120	(factory, offices, etc.)
_____	100	(equipment)
Total fixed assets	560	
_____		(items used by the company in their ordinary work)
_____		(substances for use in manufacturing)
_____	140	(value of goods being manufactured)
_____		(manufactured goods ready for sale)
_____	35	(persons owing money to the company)
_____	35	(money deposited at bank)
Total current assets	210	
_____		(debts which the company must pay in the next accounting period)
_____	50	(people owed money)
_____	30	(money owed to the bank)
_____	30	(taxes)
Total current liabilities	110	
Net current assets	100	
Net assets	660	

---

asset/assets	debtor/debtors
balance sheet/balances sheet	finished good/finished goods
bank overdraft/bank overdrafts	fix asset/fixed assets
building/buildings	land/lands
cash in hand at bank/cashes in hand at bank	plant and machinery/plant and machineries
creditor/creditors	raw material/raw materials
current asset/current assets	taxation/taxations
current liability/current liabilities	work in progress/works in progress

See LOBE:
Unit 48 – Nouns
Unit 49 – Noun compounds
Unit 50 – Genitive forms

Exercise 1

Correct or improve the following expressions, where necessary.

1   a decisions-maker
2   the decision of the board
3   an informations gathering meeting
4   useful advices
5   the fax of yesterday
6   five equipments
7   a prices quotation
8   the sale manager
9   the minutes of the secretary
10   the company results

Exercise 2

Put the apostrophe in the correct position in the following text.

Yesterdays proceedings, starting with the companys extraordinary meeting, were held in the visitors meeting room. The mornings agenda started with the Chairmans introductory speech, confirming that the first two quarters results had been better than expected. 'Its with great pleasure that I present these figures; I hadnt expected them to be quite so good.' The shareholders views were well represented by some 250 participants. The shareholders main concerns were with the companys plans to diversify into new areas such as software development. George Armstrong felt that the companys strength was its very weakness. 'I wouldnt move into new areas now; theres a lot of consolidation to be done first.' However, the Chairman, emphasising the need to take the initiative, pointed to other firms successes in these areas, particularly last months launch of Microms Opsys 95, claimed to be every organisations solution to system crashes. The members views were, however, mixed.

UNIT 43

ADJECTIVES versus ADVERBS

See LOBE:
Unit 51 – Adjectives versus adverbs

Exercise 1

Give the corresponding adverbs for the following adjectives.

1 interesting
2 economy
3 rapid
4 gradual

5 dramatic
6 good
7 healthy
8 excellent

Exercise 2

Underline six mistakes in the newspaper extract below. Then correct them.

Tourism and the price of money

The economical case for increasing investment in tourism is good, but the most recently figures available show a slower growth in tourism in most areas. For this reason, we should introduce changes gradual and only with careful consideration of future trends. An important factor will be exchange rates. With a strong currency, we can expect fewer foreign visitors. As tourism becomes increasing important, the government should think about the effects of a strongly currency on tourism and employment in the touristic industry.

Exercise 3

Choose the correct alternative to complete the sentences below.

1 The use of recycled paper is ecologicalistically/ecologically/ecologic desirable.
2 Economical/Economically/Economic considerations are also important.
3 Recycled paper is often cheap/cheaply/cheapish.
4 Most companies report a highly/high/highing level of interest in environmental issues.
5 Consumers prefer to think they are kindly/kind/kindling to animals.
6 Consumers hardly/hard/harder notice the small print on a bottle of shampoo.

Exercise 4

Look at the graph showing the decline in grain output and the decrease in the use of chemical fertilisers. Fill in the spaces in the text below with words from the box.

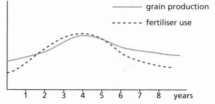

```
———— grain production
- - - - fertiliser use

  1  2  3  4  5  6  7  8  years
```

environmental   naturally
broken   economic   first
wholly   traditional   chemical
mainly   considerable

The _____ thing you can notice here is the _____ fall in grain production over the past four years. This is almost _____ due to a return to _____ farming methods. You can see, for example, that the _____ line shows a drop in the use of _____ fertilisers. This change in farming methods, _____ as a consequence of _____ pressure, has affected agricultural production in several areas. It has had important _____ effects on the farmers.

ADJECTIVE MODIFICATION with ADVERBS

See LOBE:
Unit 52 – Adjective modification with adverbs

Exercise 1

Modify the opinions expressed in the following conversation about a trade fair by adding adverbs from the box.

> extremely   reasonably   virtually   quite   fairly

Helga: Was it a _____ successful fair?

Ulrike: Well, yes, it was _____ a worthwhile couple of days. We made some _____ unexpected contacts.

Helga: So, good news! Some new business?

Ulrike: Yes, in fact, some areas where we're _____ unknown.

Helga: Good, because without new contacts these fairs can be an _____ expensive exercise.

Exercise 2

Say which of the following sentences are right and which are wrong. Correct those that are wrong.

1 The latest semi-conductors are absolutely small.
2 The amount of information that can be included on a chip is totally enormous.
3 The cost of hardware is fairly lower than it used to be.
4 Every year brings considerably significant improvements in system capability.
5 A moderately improved hardware configuration can bring important benefits.

Exercise 3

Read the following extract from a Chairman's speech to a shareholders' Annual General Meeting. Fill in the spaces with appropriate adverbs. The first letter of each one is already given.

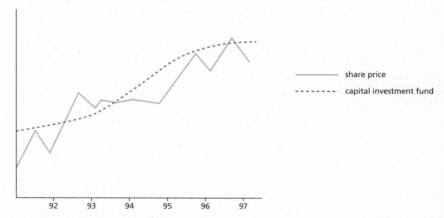

'The continued rise in our share price has been v _____ beneficial to the board, enabling us to raise money for further capital investment. This has been e _____ useful, giving us a better basis for future growth. The stock market has noticed our h _____ prudent investment policies. And consequently, investors have felt q _____ confident about our ability to give a good return on their investments. All of this proves that we are r _____ justified in expecting further success in the future.'

UNIT 45

COMPARISON of ADJECTIVES; ADJECTIVE MODIFICATION with ADVERBS

See LOBE:
Unit 52 – Adjective modification with adverbs
Unit 53 – Comparison of adjectives

Exercise 1

Arrow and Harry's are two confectionery manufacturers. Both companies have reported increased turnover and improved share price. Harry's has performed better than Arrow. Look at the table below comparing the two companies. Make 10 sentences comparing each company's performance this year with last year and comparing the two companies.

	Share price		Turnover	
	Last year	This year	Last year	This year
Arrow	£0.43	£0.48	£256m	£262m
Harry's	£0.50	£0.78	£250m	£293m

Here are two example sentences:

Arrow has a slightly improved share price.

Harry's has been much more successful than Arrow this year.

Exercise 2

Read the following newspaper report on a discussion with the Chairman of National Gas. Then write the Chairman's answers in the dialogue he had with the journalist.

Gas is best, claims NG chief

The Chairman of National Gas claimed yesterday that gas was a much more economical source of power than alternative methods of energy supply. Paul Kelving, who last year was reported to have wanted National Gas to buy shares in Wind Power, the largest alternative energy supply company, said that wind farms did not offer a better alternative to gas, being both more expensive and more destructive. Wind farms were 'ugly and no-one wanted them', said Mr Kelving. He added that gas had greatly improved the environment. Gas was much cleaner than coal and considerably safer than nuclear power.

J: How do you compare gas as a source of power with alternative methods
      of energy generation?

PK: Well, gas is _____ than alternative forms.

J: Isn't wind _____ alternative?

PK: No, wind isn't _____ . It is much _____ and _____ of the
      environment. Wind farms are ugly, no-one wants them.

J: So do you think more gas-fired power can actually improve the environment?

PK: Yes, gas is certainly _____ coal and _____ nuclear power.

J: Well, thank you, Mr Kelving.

MODIFICATION of ADVERBS; EXPRESSIONS of FREQUENCY

See LOBE:
Unit 52 – Adjective modification with adverbs
Unit 53 – Comparison of adjectives
Unit 54 – Expressions of frequency

Exercise 1

The graph below compares costs of various means of transporting goods for Tallis & Co., a white goods distributor.

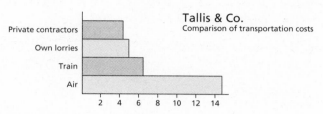

Tallis & Co.
Comparison of transportation costs

Are the following sentences true or false?

1 Using private contractors is much cheaper than using Tallis's own lorries.
2 Air transport is marginally more expensive than using trains.
3 Trains are significantly more expensive than using Tallis's lorries.
4 By far the most expensive transport method is by private contractor.
5 For Tallis & Co., road transport is generally cheaper than rail.
6 Using Tallis's own lorries is slightly more expensive than using private contractors but a great deal cheaper than using air transport.
7 Using the train is substantially cheaper than air transport.

Exercise 2

Match the frequency expression on the left with the correct meaning on the right.

1	fortnightly	a	every day
2	annually	b	every three months
3	quarterly	c	every six months
4	twice yearly	d	every year
5	daily	e	every two weeks

Exercise 3

The following extract is part of an interview with a Marketing Director of a do-it-yourself products manufacturer. She is talking about promotion methods. Complete the text with appropriate frequency and comparison words. The first letter of each missing word is given.

I: What sort of promotion usually works best for your type of goods, for DIY products?

MD: Well, first of all, we r _____ use on-pack promotions. We find that there are

        m _____ e _____ ways to promote our products. We u _____ have in-

        store demonstrations, so customers can see exactly how the product works. This makes a

        g _____ impression.

I: What about competitions, or free offers?

MD: No, we n _____ use methods like that. That might be okay for c _____ goods,

        but ours are high-quality products. The customer knows that if he or she wants the best,

        then they pay for it, but there are s _____ any extras. It's the best product to do the

        job. Simply that!

See LOBE:
Unit 55 – Degree with **very**, **too** and **enough**
Unit 56 – **So** versus **such**

Exercise 1

Complete the following letter about an invoice using the words in the box.

> very   too   so far as   enough   such   so

Dankix (Europe)
Ringstr. 13, D-3296 Bonn, Germany

Bresson & Cie
320 Rue de la Croix-Rouge   23 October 19…
75016 PARIS

Dear Sir or Madam,

Re. Our invoice No TR3487   Amount outstanding: $6,743

_____ we are aware, we have not been paid for the above
invoice. If you are unhappy about our invoice for some reason,
please call us to discuss the problem. Unfortunately, we have now
waited long _____. It is _____ a long time since we sent
the invoice and the payment is _____ late, that we are forced
to consider legal action. I am sure you would not wish to incur
_____ high legal fees on top of the amount already owed.

Since we are always prepared to help our customers, you may be
interested to know that it is not _____ late to negotiate
different payment terms. Please contact us to discuss this option.

Yours faithfully,

P. Krankl

Accounts Department

Exercise 2

Below is part of a report on a prototype design for a child's bicycle. Rewrite the sentences using the words in brackets.

Report on BX200 Prototype » » » » » » » » » »

Conclusions

1 The distance between the handlebar and the brake is too small. (enough/wide)

2 The saddle is 12 cms wide; it should be 15 cms. (too/narrow)

3 The rubber on the handlebars is too hard. (enough/soft)

4 The frame is very light but it is sufficiently strong. (It is surprising/such/so)

5 The high-quality materials may demand an impossible retail price. (such/too high).

6 The improvements have to be made quickly, so the bike will be ready for Christmas. (So long as)

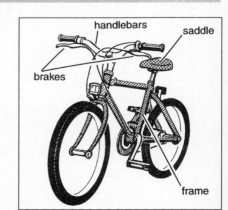

COMPARISON OF ADJECTIVES; ALREADY, YET, AGAIN and STILL

See LOBE:
Unit 53 – Comparison of adjectives
Unit 57 – **Already, yet, again** and **still**

Exercise 1

Look at the graph from a sales report showing the sales for three laptop computers. Then complete the summary using the graph to help you. The first letter of each word you need is given.

Sales of A,B,C since launch

1   Model A has always been t _____ b _____ seller. After one year, A had a _____ reached 300 and sales rose in the second year and a _____ last year. However, A has probably a _____ peaked, but we do expect that next year it will sell a _____ much a _____ this year.

2   Sales of model B started well and were a _____ at 300 by last year. Although sales are s _____ at 300 units this year, they are expected to rise a _____ next year.

3   Model C has always been t _____ w _____ performer. Sales have a _____ fallen and will fall a _____ next year. We have not y _____ made a decision on future marketing of C, but it has always sold l _____ t _____ we expected, so we may drop it.

Comparison of Sales:
Laptop computer models A, B, C.

——— actual sales

- - - - - forecast sales

Exercise 2

The following letter is from a food manufacturer to a magazine editor. It concerns information given on food packaging. Complete the text with appropriate words from the box.

> again   yet   still   already   as soon as

Veggie foods ltd

Croydon Lane, East Grimstead, SU3 5TR

P. Payne
League for Consumer Protection
20 Epping Way
London SE23 6TR

13 August 19...

Dear Mr Payne

Thank you for your letter concerning the information given on our food packaging. You will be glad to know that in line with government regulations we _____ give detailed lists of ingredients on all the packaging of our products. We do not _____ provide details of how the foods are produced but we do have plans to give this information as well. We are _____ involved in research to find the best way to give this information. _____ we reach a decision, we will begin labelling all our foods with details of where and how the foods are produced.

Once _____ , thank you for your concern.

Best wishes,

Anna Foboff,
Public Relations

Exercise 1

Here are some notes about a typical day in the life of Paul Davies, a leading industrialist.
Expand the notes, adding articles, where necessary.

> If I am at home, I get up at 6.30.
> I wash; then I go for jog before breakfast.
> After jog, shower.
> Breakfast – usually bowl of cereal.
> During breakfast, I read newspaper.
> Car from garage and drive to office.
> Journey takes about 20 minutes.
> At office, first look at post and e-mail.
> Very good secretary who plans and organises timetable for me.
> I travel to Spain about three times/month.
> I like working with Spanish because they enjoy life – both professional and social side.
> In Madrid I often go to theatre or concert.
> At home, evening I usually watch TV news before going to bed.

Exercise 2

Sumita are just about to launch their new ten-speed CD-ROM drive on the market. Their technical
documentation team are writing the final section for the manual on troubleshooting. Complete the
text by adding articles, where necessary.

Section 6

Sumita CD-ROM drives are designed to provide countless hours of trouble-free operation without maintenance, However, problems do sometimes occur, though most of them are easy to solve without great deal of technical expertise. So, if problem does occur, first step is to make sure that software has been properly installed; you will see error message on screen when you start up machine if something has not been correctly installed. If problem persists, check following items:

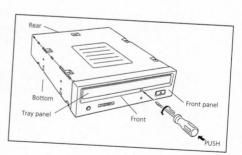

If disc tray does not open:

■ is power cord connected?
  is power switch turned to ON position?
  You will see short flash of light from front panel when drive is powered up.
  Remember that disc tray will not move without supplying power.

■ If disc tray does not move even when power is supplied, turn power switch to OFF position and turn emergency knob in anti-clockwise direction while pressing with small screwdriver. Then disc tray will open little way. Carefully pull disc tray open and close disc tray again.

■ After closing disc tray, turn power switch to ON and check tray operates correctly.

If tray now operates correctly, insert disc and read ***section 4*** in booklet.

And remember, discs should always be stored in their cases when not in use to keep them free from dirt and dust.

Exercise 1

Add articles, where necessary, in the following business quotes.

1   International business may conduct its operations with scraps of paper, but ink it uses is human blood.
(Eric Ambler, b. 1909, British novelist)

2   Executives are like joggers. If you stop jogger, he goes on running on spot. If you drag executive away from his business, he goes on running on spot, pawing ground, talking business.
(Jean Baudrillard, b. 1929, French semiologist)

3   Corporation. Ingenious device for obtaining individual profit without individual responsibility.
(Ambrose Bierce, 1842–1914, US author)

4   It is interest of commercial world that wealth should be found everywhere.
(Edmund Burke, 1729–97, Irish philosopher and statesman)

5   Client is to me mere unit, factor in problem.
(Sir Arthur Conan Doyle, 1859–1930, English author)

6   It is very vulgar to talk about one's business. Only people like stockbrokers do that, and then merely at dinner parties.
(Oscar Wilde, 1854–1900, Anglo-Irish playwright and author)

7   What's good for country is good for General Motors, and vice versa.
(Charles Wilson, 1890–1961, US industrialist, Secretary of Defense)

Exercise 2

Anna Singer is preparing for her business law exams and is testing herself on key terms. First match the legal terms (1–10) with their definitions (a–j); then add articles, where necessary, to make definitions in complete sentences. The first one has been done for you.

1	contract	6	judgement
2	crime	7	merger
3	damages	8	premium
4	duty	9	remuneration
5	goods	10	title

a   joining together of two companies under name of one of them or as new company
b   actual decision of court in particular case which settles outcome of case and binds parties to dispute
c   subject matter of contract for sale of goods
d   wrong done to State which is dealt with by means of prosecution
e   price paid by insured person in insurance contract
f   financial compensation awarded to innocent party for breach of duty
g   legal ownership of property by one person
h   agreement between two parties, which is based on offer by one and acceptance by other
i   obligation owed by one person to another
j   payment of sum of money in exchange for services

Example:

*1 h A contract is **an** agreement between two parties, which is based on **an** offer by one and **an** acceptance by **the** other.*

UNIT 51

PRONOUNS

See LOBE:
Unit 59 – Pronouns

Exercise 1

Circle the 'odd one out' in the following groups.

1	I	me	myself	your	mine
2	it	it's	itself	its	hers
3	theirselves	they	themselves	them	their
4	we	you	he	she	me
5	our	your	there	her	its

Exercise 2

Complete the following dialogue between Andrew, Boris and Sylvia about the launch of a new shampoo, using suitable pronouns.

Andrew: _____ 'm not totally convinced about _____ new packaging. What do _____ think about _____ , Sylvia?

Sylvia: _____ 'm reasonably happy with _____ , _____ . _____ think the caption captures what _____ are trying to say with _____ new product. A family product – no frills. _____ think _____ 'll appeal to _____ target shopper and _____ 'll put _____ straight into _____ supermarket trolley. OK, the bottle _____ is nothing special, but in any case _____ are aiming at the average consumer.

Andrew: Yes, but _____ average consumer has become a lot more demanding. _____ are looking for products with a distinctive style and _____ just doesn't stand out from the crowd.

Boris: So what do _____ suggest?

Andrew: _____ think _____ are going to have to rethink the packaging. If _____ look at WashWell and Fresh Hair, _____ are both clearly identifiable by _____ packaging. _____ have always prided _____ on staying ahead of the competition. So, _____ can't let _____ overtake _____ now. So, _____ recommend that _____ talk to the design team again and ask _____ to come up with a new bottle and new packaging. This is a really important product for _____ and _____ can't afford to make any mistakes. If _____ like, _____ 'll talk to _____ _____ . _____ 'll contact Pete Menzies first; _____ usually has some innovative ideas.

Boris: Yes, _____ think that's a good idea to ask _____ . So, please keep _____ informed of developments.

Exercise 3

Homecare have prepared this promotional letter to send in a mail shot with their new catalogue, but it needs editing. Put the sentences into the correct order.

- As for delivery, they'll be with you next day. ( )
- HomeCare is a leading name in products for the home. ( )
- In short, you'll find something for everyone. ( )
- It contains a wealth of new ideas to improve the look of your house. ( )
- Our products are not available on the high street. ( )
- So, phone us today and improve your major asset. ( )
- That's our promise. ( )
- There are also many new products for those of you who are already experts. ( )
- These include easy-to-install tips for the novice. ( )
- We are pleased to send you our latest catalogue of home improvements. ( )
- You can only buy them through this catalogue. ( )

See LOBE:
Unit 59 – Pronouns
Unit 60 – Demonstratives

Exercise 1

Read through the following letter. Circle the pronouns and demonstratives, then link them to the phrases they refer to. The first has been done as an example.

Communication Consultants
135 Broad Street
Debenham
DB12 5TY
Tel: +44 15687 678789
Fax: +44 15687 234634

Mr Markku Savonen
ICD Systems OY
PO Box 345
FIN-00101 Helsinki 12
FINLAND
22/09/95

Mr Savonen and Paul Roberts

Dear Mr Savonen

Further to our recent phone conversation about training programmes, I have pleasure in sending you our brochure. This presents the range of training services we provide. Solutions vary from client to client, but all our programmes are composed of the following elements:

skills-building programmes: these aim to develop **communication skills,** for example in presentations, meetings and negotiations. Participants on this type of course typically come from the same department. It is important that their language level is roughly homogeneous.

cross-cultural programmes: these focus on the **individual, their company and its culture.** Participants in these workshops develop their awareness of their own culture and explore its impact on their working methods.

team-building programmes: these investigate the characteristics of **teams:** why some of them succeed and others fail. By the end of this seminar individuals will have a better understanding of their strengths and weaknesses.

I hope this information is of interest to you and I look forward to speaking to you again once the needs of your managers have been more clearly defined. Finally, please feel free to contact me if you would like to discuss any of these programmes in more detail.

Yours sincerely

Paul Roberts

Paul Roberts
Partner

Exercise 2

Rewrite the following dialogue using appropriate pronouns and demonstratives to replace the underlined words.

A: Primebuild are recruiting engineers for a construction project in SE Asia.

B: Who are <u>Primebuild</u>?

A: <u>Primebuild</u> design and construct power plants.

B: But do <u>Primebuild</u> install <u>the plants</u>?

A: No, <u>Primebuild</u> do all the initial construction work for water and electricity. After <u>the initial construction work</u> is completed, the power generators install the <u>real</u> equipment.

B: And <u>the</u> engineers <u>that you mentioned</u> … where are <u>the engineers</u> to work exactly?

A: <u>The</u> advertisement <u>I have here</u> just says SE Asia.

B: Yes, but <u>SE Asia</u> is a very large area.

A: Yes, I know <u>what you mean</u>. But, to be honest, I'd be happy to get a job somewhere away from <u>the</u> area <u>around here.</u> <u>The area</u> has too many unhappy memories for me. I've applied for too many jobs …

B: … and got none of <u>the jobs</u>. I know <u>the</u> feeling <u>you have</u>. In fact maybe I <u>too</u> will apply.

UNIT 53

SOME, ANY and RELATED WORDS (1)

See LOBE:
Unit 61 – **Some, any** and related words (1)
Unit 62 – **Some, any** and related words (2)

Exercise 1

*Complete the following sentences with **some**, **any** or a related word/phrase.*

1 Let me give you _____ advice.
2 I can't find _____ information about the company.
3 I'll look _____ else. It could be in another file.
4 Have you _____ been to the Trade Fair in Dortmund?
5 I was _____ confused by his presentation. It just didn't make _____ sense.
6 We'll _____ use that supplier again. They let us down terribly.

Exercise 2

*Jane Gaymer has just given a presentation on the future of the coal industry and is waiting for questions from the audience. Complete this extract by adding **some**, **any** or a related word/phrase.*

Jane: Thank you very much for your attention. And now, are there _____ questions?
Peter: Jane, do you think that prices will _____ return to their pre-1980 level?
Jane: Thanks for your question. In fact, I am not _____ surprised by your concern about prices. But I am sure that prices will _____ return to those levels. The current situation of over-supply means that customers can buy stocks almost _____ from their traditional suppliers. In fact, having spoken to _____ of them recently, they have told me they have reached the stage where there is _____ to store the surplus coal they have mined. And they simply can't do _____ to influence the situation. In the history of the industry, we've seen _____ like this before. Of course, _____ could happen in the future, but I think we have to be pragmatic. So, to answer your question, _____ return to earlier prices! I know that that is not _____ you like to hear, but I think it sums up the present situation. Does that answer your question?
Peter: Yes, thanks.
Jane: _____ more questions?
        (No hands go up)
        I'm sure there are _____ more questions ! No? Well, if there are _____ more questions at the moment, I'd like to thank you for your attention, and please feel free to contact me if you'd like to discuss _____ of the points I raised. In _____ case, I'll be seeing _____ of you _____ later today in our small working groups.

Exercise 3

*Complete the following telephone dialogue by adding **some**, **any** or a related word/phrase.*

A: Could you put me through to _____ in your accounts department, please.
B: Is there _____ in particular you'd like to speak to?
A: No, but it's in connection with _____ bills we have received.
B: Just one moment, and I'll connect you to Mr Kempton. (Pause)
     I'm afraid there's _____ there at the moment. But, if you hold, I'll just check if I can find him _____ in the building.
A: Actually, I've got _____ other phone calls to make now. So, I'd appreciate if you could ask _____ to phone me.
B: _____ particular time?
A: _____ time this afternoon, please.
B: Fine, I'll do that.
A: Can you give me your name, please?
B: Yes, it's …

SOME, ANY and RELATED WORDS (2)

See LOBE:
Unit 61 – **Some, any** and related words (1)
Unit 62 – **Some, any** and related words (2)

Exercise 1

Are the following sentences right or wrong? If wrong, correct them.

1 We are not interested in a new equipment at the moment.
2 Let me give you some advice.
3 I haven't told somebody yet about the new contract.
4 Any of the new employees would be able to tell you the exact figure.
5 Does anyone have any questions?
6 Don't do nothing until you have spoken to a lawyer.

Exercise 2

Kray Associates are having problems with their computers. So they ring the help line to try to solve the problem. Complete the dialogue by selecting the appropriate response from the box below.

HL: Is there any message on screen when you start the system?

_____

HL: And does it say anything after that?

_____

HL: And has any new software been installed on the system?

_____

HL: And does anyone apart from the authorised users use the system?

_____

KA: So, is there anything that you can do to solve the problem over the phone?

_____

KA: So, when can you send someone over?

_____

KA: We really need someone to come over today.

_____

HL: OK, I'll make sure we send someone over some time this afternoon.
HL: If you hang on, I'll just check if we have anyone anywhere in your area.
KA: Yes, it says 'virus detected'.
HL: No, I don't think so.
KA: Yes, then it says 'Do you want to continue?'
KA: No, absolutely nothing.
KA: No, no-one at all.

Exercise 3

*August Dermassey is at customs at Rotaronga International Airport and is being questioned by a customs official. Complete the following dialogue by writing **some, any** or a related word/phrase.*

CO: Good morning, sir. Could I see your passport, please?
AD: Yes, here you are.
CO: Have you _____ visited Rotaronga before?
AD: No, I've _____ been here before.
CO: And is this all your luggage? Do you have _____ else?
AD: No, this is everything.
CO: And are you carrying _____ for _____ else?
AD: No, this is all mine.
CO: Do you have _____ to declare? _____ wine, spirits, cigarettes?
AD: No, _____ .
CO: Fine. And have you booked _____ to stay here in Rotaronga?
AD: No, not yet. I was hoping to book _____ downtown from the airport.
CO: Actually, as far as I know, _____ of the big hotels have any spare rooms, but it just so happens that my brother runs a nice clean pension very close to the centre. Are you _____ interested? Anyway, here's his card.

UNIT 55

QUANTIFIERS (1)

See LOBE:
Unit 61 – **Some, any** and related words (1)
Unit 63 – Quantifiers (1)
Unit 64 – Quantifiers (2)

Exercise 1

Correct the mistakes in the following sentences about textiles.

1 We produce all the kinds of textiles.
2 The most of them are made from natural products.
3 Many of raw materials come from New Zealand.
4 How many do you pay per tonne?
5 The price depends on a lots of different factors.
6 In the past we used to pay just a few money for synthetics, but this has increased a lot recently.
7 Of course, we have several of competitors.
8 Only a little of them are in this country, because labour costs here are so high.
9 We don't expect no further price increases in raw materials this year.

Exercise 2

Paula Ronzoni is trying to install the new version of Opsys on her computer. As she is getting error messages on the screen, she rings the computer help line. The technical support department talk her through the installation procedure. Complete the phone call with an appropriate word/phrase from the box below. Use each word/phrase once.

HL: So is there _____ message on the screen?

PR: Yes, it says 'Do you have _____ other version of Opsys on your system?'

HL: And do you?

PR: No, I have _____ version of Opsys at all.

HL: So, press 'enter'.

PR: Now it says 'You have too _____ disk space for installation.'

HL: How _____ disk space does it say you have?

PR: 2.4 megabytes.

HL: Then you'll have to delete _____ programs to make disk space. Do you have _____ backup files on your hard disk?

PR: Yes, I think I have _____ .

HL: Well, you don't need those. You can delete _____ of them.

PR: OK, I'll do that now. Can you wait _____ while?

HL: Yes.

PR: Right, I've deleted _____ of them.

HL: So, now key in 'install' again and let's see if you can load Opsys.

PR: Right. Yes, it's working. Now it shows '25 per cent installed'.

HL: So, it's installed _____ of the files.

PR: Now 50 per cent ... now 75 per cent.

HL: Right, that's _____ of the files.

PR: Now 100 per cent.

HL: Good, so that's _____ of it installed.

PR: Thanks for your help.

many	little	a lot
any	most	all
no	a few	any
all	much	a little
all	a few	

See LOBE:
Unit 61 – **Some, any** and related words (1)
Unit 62 – **Some, any** and related words (2)
Unit 63 – Quantifiers (1)
Unit 64 – Quantifiers (2)

Exercise 1

Which option, a, b or c, has the closest meaning to each numbered sentence?

1 Not all our products meet our quality requirements.
  a All of our products fail the quality tests.
  b Most of our products fail the quality test.
  c Some of our products fail the quality tests.

2 However, most of our products meet our customers' requirements.
  a Some of our products fall below our customers' requirements.
  b Only a few of our products fall below our customers' requirements.
  c None of our products falls below our customers' requirements.

3 We only receive a few complaints about product quality.
  a We don't get any complaints about product quality.
  b We don't get many complaints about product quality.
  c We don't get several complaints about product quality.

4 No customer complaint is unanswered.
  a We reply to all customer complaints.
  b We reply to most customer complaints.
  c We reply to many customer complaints.

5 Many companies pay too little attention to customer service.
  a Most companies don't take enough care of their customers.
  b A lot of companies don't take enough care of their customers.
  c Some companies take enough care of their customers.

Exercise 2

Homelec are having a problem with their Tantra washing machine, so they have put the following notice in the newspaper. Complete the announcement with suitable quantifiers.

IMPORTANT NOTICE

It has come to our notice that a very _____ of the Tantra models sold over the last few months may have _____ problem with their electrical wiring. We would like to emphasise that _____ of the products are defect-free and this problem affects only _____ models. However, we have decided to recall _____ the Tantra models with serial numbers from A56000 to B12000. In _____ cases, you will find this number at the back of the machine; in the newer models it is on the side. Finally, let me reassure _____ our customers that this fault poses _____ danger whatever and we are recalling them merely as a precaution.

Please call one of the following numbers so that we can arrange collection.

North	Central	South
0161-456-4567	**0121-098-4120**	**0171-067-7548**

Exercise 3

Below is a list of the typical problems that users may have with their Constant Colour Jet 340 printer. Which remedy (a–f) goes with which problem (1–6)?

1 No print
2 Indicator light, no print
3 Error lights blinking
4 Paper doesn't load
5 Paper jams
6 Poor print quality

a Set lever to correct position. NOTE: Don't try to put in too much paper.

b Clean print head several times by pressing 'clean' button. A few ink cartridges have blockages preventing ink from firing. If problem persists, exchange ink cartridge.

c Check that all the leads are connected and that all the indicators light up when machine is switched on.
If nothing happens, contact your service representative.

d If these stay on and bleeper sounds several times, turn off your printer. Wait a few minutes. Then turn printer on again. If problem persists after several attempts, contact your service representative for assistance.

e Make sure that you have loaded all the correct software for your printer and that you have put some paper into the printer.

f Switch off power. Open front cover. Remove paper.

UNIT 57

EACH, EVERY and COMPOUNDS; QUANTIFIERS

See LOBE:
Unit 66 – **Each** and **every**
Unit 67 – Compounds with **every**
Unit 63 – Quantifiers (1)
Unit 64 – Quantifiers (2)

Exercise 1

Find 12 words belonging to these groups in the word box opposite.

E	V	E	R	Y	O	N	E	B	A	L	L
G	I	L	B	N	O	O	F	S	T	R	I
C	O	P	E	R	T	B	T	R	L	O	T
N	I	T	I	N	N	O	N	E	A	S	T
B	R	E	R	F	O	D	A	S	N	P	L
P	O	E	V	E	R	Y	W	H	E	R	E
N	U	A	R	W	Z	O	I	Y	V	A	R
M	U	C	H	F	R	U	I	T	E	T	R
R	M	H	O	P	S	E	V	E	R	A	L

Exercise 2

*Rewrite the following sentences replacing the underlined words with a phrase including **each, every** or a compound, and making any other necessary grammatical changes.*

1 We have been selling our products <u>in all countries</u> in Europe for many years now.
2 <u>Both</u> of our European subsidiaries have been very successful in entering new markets.
3 <u>All the people</u> in our European offices are linked via a local area network.
4 <u>All the</u> senior managers receive regular training in the latest management techniques.
5 I am very surprised that <u>on all the occasions</u> I visit head office, I meet new personnel.
6 We feel that we have carried out <u>all the</u> necessary <u>jobs</u> to secure the future survival of the firm.
7 We prepare management accounts in <u>March, June, September and December</u>.
8 <u>All</u> of our employees are encouraged to contribute to the suggestions scheme.

Exercise 3

As companies become more and more international in their activities, they need to be able to move their employees to business units around the world. Below is a letter to employees about appraisal and relocation. Combine the first halves of the sentences with the phrases below to produce a memo to employees about the new appraisal system.

Memo

To: all Grade II
From: HR

1   We are writing to all employees _____
2   Over the last six months _____
3   We have now collated all the details _____
4   This systematisation will enable all employees _____
5   We expect that this increased mobility will lead to benefits _____
6   Of course we do not intend to relocate employees _____
7   And that is why these appraisal interviews are crucial. _____

a   every time it suits the company's interests.
b   and every procedure has been systematised to produce a single homogeneous system.
c   because they will enable each of you to discuss your career objectives with your superiors.
d   to inform everyone about the new appraisal system.
e   to move easily between each of the company's overseas business units.
f   we have visited each of our subsidiaries to collect information about their procedures.
g   everywhere in the company.

See LOBE:
Unit 68 – Numerals

Exercise 1

Write the following words in alphanumeric format.

1 one thousand, four hundred and forty six
2 three and three quarters
3 eighty five point seven six two
4 the twenty third of April nineteen ninety-nine (various possibilities)
5 twenty five minutes to seven in the evening (various possibilities)
6 one million dollars
7 five point seven billion pounds
8 eight metres by four metres
9 twenty five plus sixteen equals forty one
10 eight squared
11 the square root of eight
12 nine to the power twenty five

Exercise 2

Look at the following plan for a bridge to link the island of Spuria to the mainland of Rotaronga. Then complete the overhead projector transparency for the engineer's presentation.

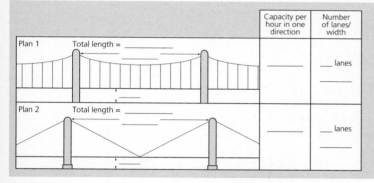

	Capacity per hour in one direction	Number of lanes/ width
Plan 1 Total length = _____	_____	_____ lanes
Plan 2 Total length = _____	_____	_____ lanes

Plan 1 is for a structure 36 kilometres in length. If you look at your diagrams, you will see it will have 6 motorway lanes. Each lane will be a standard 4 metres wide. There will be one for slow-moving traffic and the other two for overtaking. Our calculation is that these lanes will carry an estimated 6000 vehicles per hour in each direction. The structure will consist of 7 spans, each of which will be 5 kilometres apart. And finally, you can see that the structure will be built at a height of 70 metres above sea level.

Moving on to plan 2, this is for a construction also 36 kilometres in length at a height of 65 metres above sea level. It will consist of 48 spans and each span will be 850 metres in length. The bridge will have 4 lanes and will carry 3000 vehicles per hour in each direction. Again we plan to construct each lane to a width of 4 metres, making a total of 16 metres.

Exercise 3

Susanne Meier has just returned to her office after a marketing trip to Malaysia. She turns on her ansaphone and hears the following messages. Complete her notes in numeric form.

1 Marketing meeting scheduled for sixteenth February at two o'clock in room four. Expected to last two hours. Please confirm you can attend by phoning extension ninety three, forty six.
    Marketing meeting on _____ at _____ in _____ . Call ext. _____ .

2 Problems with new brochure – too many words. If we use standard A four, then we can have one hundred and twenty words per page; if we increase height of page by three centimetres, then we can have one hundred and fifty words per page. By the way, do you want subheadings in round brackets or square brackets?
    Brochure: _____ ; _____ . Subheadings: _____ or _____ ?

3 New shelving for your office to be delivered on eighteenth February after nine o'clock. Dimensions are three point five metres wide, two point eight metres in length and thirty centimetres deep. Please ring five six two seven three one if this time is not convenient.
    Delivery on _____ after _____ . Dimensions: _____ Ring _____ .

4 Don't understand your marketing expenses. Your receipts are for one hundred and twenty French francs, two thousand six hundred Spanish pesetas and twelve thousand four hundred and sixty Italian lire. This does not convert to five hundred and sixteen pounds. Please ring accounts.
    Marketing receipts: _____

UNIT 59

TIME (1)

See LOBE:
Unit 69 – Time (1)
Unit 70 – Time (2)

Exercise 1

Identify 10 time prepositions in the following word box. You can read four words horizontally, five vertically and one diagonally.

B	E	T	W	E	E	N
Y	E	G	X	Z	F	P
D	A	F	T	E	R	N
U	R	R	O	T	O	M
R	G	I	N	R	M	S
I	K	X	L	O	E	B
N	G	H	A	A	N	C
G	U	N	T	I	L	A

Exercise 2

Look at the following project plan for the launch of a new product. Complete the extract from the project leader's briefing by adding words from the list in the box. You will need to use some words twice.

> during   in   by   between   beginning   on   before

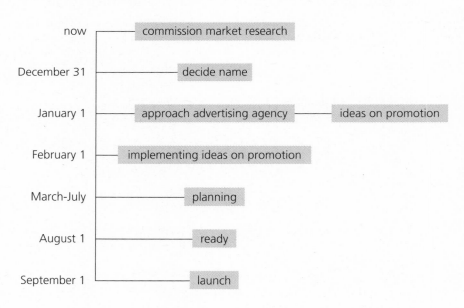

'_____ we can decide on a name for the product we shall have to commission some market research. It is important that we decide this _____ the _____ of January because _____ the whole of January we will be talking to an advertising agency about ideas on how to promote the product _____ time for the autumn season. _____ February 1, we will begin discussions on implementation of ideas. Then _____ March and July we will turn ideas into firm strategy. Everything will be ready _____ August 1 for the launch _____ September.'

See LOBE:
Unit 69 – Time (1)
Unit 70 – Time (2)

Exercise 1

Read the following extract from a newspaper article on changes in the world car industry. Complete the text with appropriate words. The first letter of each missing word is given.

Japanese pressure improves design

D _____ the 1970s the European car industry was in crisis. A _____ several difficult years t _____ the 1980s, with a lot of reorganisation and jobs lost, the industry changed dramatically. Not only were the major manufacturers in better economic and industrial health, but f _____ the b _____ of the 1990s cars were better designed and more reliable. One reason for this improvement was that d _____ the 1980s there was strong competition from the Pacific Rim, and Japan in particular. The emphasis was on quality and reliability. F _____ the early 1980s t _____ the present, there has been a revolution in the performance of almost every manufacturer. Now there are still too many cars in production, but poor design and bad quality are a thing of the past.

Exercise 2

Look at the diagram showing the typical demand for electricity during 24 hours in summer and winter. Read the description that follows. Are the sentences grammatically right or wrong? If wrong, correct them.

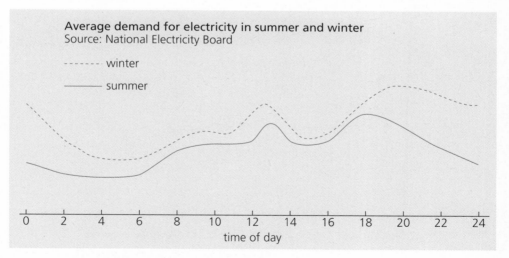

Average demand for electricity in summer and winter
Source: National Electricity Board

- - - - - - winter
—————— summer

time of day

1 While the night, there is little demand for power.
2 Then at the morning, demand rises again as people wake up and make breakfast.
3 For early morning to around midday, demand is constant, with an increase on lunchtime.
4 Through the afternoon, demand is fairly constant unto the evening when it increases as people get home from work.
5 At around teatime, the demand for electricity reaches a peak.
6 Obviously on sundown and bedtime demand remains high, especially by winter.

UNIT ◆61◆

TIME versus PLACE (1)

See LOBE:
Unit 69 – Time (1)
Unit 70 – Time (2)
Unit 71 – Place

Exercise 1

Complete the following conversation about a business trip using words from the box. You will have to use some words more than once.

| In | around | away | outside | over | to | on | close | near | after | at | from | far |

Julia: So, what's your itinerary for your Latin American trip next week?

Brian: Well, it's very busy. _____ the first day, Monday, we land _____ Peru – we'll visit two customers _____ the Callao district of Lima, _____ the port. _____ two meetings with them we'll spend the night _____ Lima, meeting them again _____ Tuesday morning if necessary. If not we can relax and go _____ a museum, or have a look _____ the city centre, or simply wait _____ the hotel if we prefer.

Julia: It doesn't sound too busy so far!

Brian: Well, there's more to come! _____ Tuesday afternoon _____ three o'clock we take a plane _____ Lima _____ Arequipa _____ the south of Peru. Here we have our main agent for the Andean region, so we're going to spend two days with him. Then we take a plane _____ the Andes, direct _____ Buenos Aires to meet our Argentinean agent…

Julia: Is he in Buenos Aires?

Brian: Well, not exactly. But not _____ _____ . About thirty kilometres _____ the city centre, but I think he has an office _____ to the centre. But our meeting will be at his ranch – _____ the city.

Julia: That sounds good! And when do you get back?

Brian: _____ May 23, _____ four o'clock in the morning!

Lima
Arequipa

Buenos Aires

Exercise 2

Match each of the prepositions in the box to one of the diagrams below.

| inside outside | through over | on top of off | to on | at into | along across | away from under |

1   2   3   4   5   6   7

8   9   10   11   12   13   14

See LOBE:
Unit 69 – Time (1)
Unit 70 – Time (2)
Unit 71 – Place

Exercise 1

Are the following sentences right or wrong? If wrong, correct them.

1   We drove right across the United States.
2   We arrived by Los Angeles in a Sunday evening.
3   We stayed by the Hotel Excelsior.
4   We walked along Hollywood Boulevard.
5   The names of all the stars are written in the concrete.
6   We then went up to San Francisco and stayed inside a friend's house.
7   We stayed there since a week.
8   At the end of the week we decided to go in Arizona.
9   We had to drive along the Nevada desert.
10   It was incredibly hot under the Nevada sun on midday.
11   We spent two weeks at Arizona.
12   We had to be home again by the end of the month.
13   We drove to Las Vegas and flew home by there.

Exercise 2

Look at the diagram of a gas turbine engine below. Then complete the description of how a gas turbine engine works. The first letter of each missing word is given.

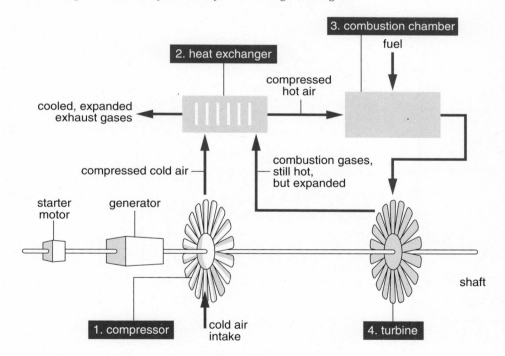

The gas turbine engine works by air passing t _____ its four main parts. First cold air enters the compressor (1). The compressor reduces the air pressure and forces air i _____ the heat exchanger (2). Hot exhaust combustion gases ensure that the temperature i _____ the heat exchanger remains high. The air is heated and then is forced t _____ the combustion chamber (3). Fuel is burned i _____ the combustion chamber, raising the temperature to 650 °C. These gases are then forced o _____ of the combustion chamber and i _____ the turbine (4). This drives the turbine.

UNIT 63

TIME versus PLACE (3)

See LOBE:
Unit 69 – Time (1)
Unit 70 – Time (2)
Unit 71 – Place

Exercise 1

Complete the following phrases by adding a suitable word. If no preposition is needed, leave the space blank.

1 I'll see you _____ the beginning of the month.
2 I'm away now _____ a few days.
3 He takes a day off _____ Christmas Day.
4 He takes three days off _____ Easter.
5 I live _____ an apartment.
6 The repair will take _____ a week.
7 I'll see you _____ the hotel lobby.
8 Do you mean _____ reception?
9 The film begins _____ 10 o'clock.
10 Is the presentation _____ the main auditorium?
11 No, you should go _____ Room 48.
12 He used to live _____ the sea.
13 He had a house _____ an island.
14 I like walking _____ beautiful cities.
15 I prefer walking _____ deserted beaches.
16 I was born _____ 1956 _____ December 30.
17 Shakespeare came _____ Stratford-on-Avon _____ England.
18 Without a visa you can't get _____ the country.
19 Without an export licence, you can't send some goods _____ _____ the country.
20 Some people can't sleep _____ night after drinking coffee.
21 Then they fall asleep _____ the day.
22 I'm going _____ home now.
23 _____ three months we move _____ a new office.
24 Can I borrow this book _____ next week?
25 I'll give it _____ you _____ Monday.
26 We won't meet _____ tomorrow. I'll see you _____ next week.

Exercise 2

Two colleagues are staying at a hotel for a meeting the next day. They are discussing the programme for the meeting. Choose the correct alternative to complete their conversation.

Diana: Before/During breakfast I'd like to have a swim.

Anna: Really?

Diana: Yes, of course! Then in/over breakfast we can meet our colleagues of/from Paris.
        In/On the morning we should have a brainstorm to identify key areas of interest.

Anna: Yes, I think so too.

Diana: For/By lunchtime we should have an agenda for the afternoon. Then we should
        go to/in a restaurant for lunch. On/At two o'clock we should begin the
        afternoon session.

Anna: Okay. Sounds okay.

Diana: I think we'll finish along/around four o'clock. So, see you at/in breakfast.
        Good night!

Exercise 1

*Look at how the words **like, as** and **such as** are used in the following sentences.*
*Label them **the same as** (S), **example** (E), **similar** (SIM), **like = as** (L/A).*

1 Companies such as BP and Shell have long experience of working in the North Sea. _____
2 Many workers in the oil industry are employed as independent contractors. _____
3 The industry has a high profile, as one would expect for such a
   multi-million dollar sector. _____
4 Health and Safety issues are regarded as primary public concerns. _____
5 Many northern European cities like Aberdeen and Stavanger have benefited from the
   oil industry. _____
6 The basic technique used to drill for oil uses a drill like that of an ordinary domestic
   power drill for making holes in walls, metal or wood. _____

Exercise 2

Read the following text about mud, or drilling fluid, used in the oil industry. Fill in the spaces with
like, as *or **such as**.*

Mud technology in drilling

In the petroleum industry, a key area of the drilling operation is known _____ mud technology.

Mud, sometimes known _____ drilling fluid, in the petroleum engineering context, is not

_____ mud for the gardener. Mud is often a complex combination of ingredients used to

circulate throughout the bore-hole, or drill-hole, during drilling. The mud works _____ a lubricant

with several other important functions, _____ the following: it cleans out the bore-hole, returns

pieces of rock to the surface, protects the sides of the bore-hole, preventing problems _____ the

sides caving in, it lubricates and cools the bit and maintains steady air pressure. Different muds are

used for different conditions. Chemicals are added to the mud so that it sets _____ jelly when

not being pumped, so avoiding problems _____ the bore-hole getting blocked up.

Usually one individual works _____ a Mud Engineer, someone who is responsible for

controlling the behaviour of the mud and checking that the drilling operation works _____ it

should. This is a key responsibility since, _____ already stated, mud is a complex and vitally

important aspect of the industry.

Exercise 3

The extract below from an internal memo concerns a dispute over recruitment in a research-based
*industry. Complete the text using **as, like** and **such as**.*

MEMORANDUM *Confidential*

Date/time: Tuesday 17.00
To: FD
From: HA

_____ you know, we need to employ people who have worked _____
top-level research scientists. Salaries have to be _____ high
_____ those in other companies _____ ours. People _____ Tom do
not understand the competition we face in recruiting top people.
_____ the candidate he thinks is too expensive.

PART ◆ 2

FUNCTIONS

CLASSIFYING INFORMATION; CONNECTING and SEQUENCING IDEAS (1)

See LOBE:
Unit 73 – Classifying information
Unit 74 – Connecting and sequencing ideas

Exercise 1

Read the following extract from a Company Director's speech to senior managers about plans to reorganise the services the company offers.

1   Identify:
   a   the existing way in which the services are categorised
   b   the proposed new way to categorise the services
2   Look at the text again. Identify:
   a   a word which indicates a statement of the obvious
   b   four expressions which indicate a time relationship
   c   two expressions which indicate a summary
   d   an expression which indicates a generalisation

'To understand the reorganisation we have to describe the present situation. Basically we operate in two different areas: new systems and modification of existing systems. We now want to change this, to a plan of four basic types of service: new systems, custom-built designs, system modification and consultancy.

In reorganising the way we describe our services, clearly the most important thing is to make sure the changes have, first of all, the support of all staff, and secondly that there are real marketing benefits. We can compare our situation now with our sister company in Rotterdam. Briefly, their plans were on the whole not popular at first, but subsequently were found to be acceptable and now, on the whole, their experience has proved extremely positive. To sum up, I'm sure we can learn from the Rotterdam experience.'

Exercise 2

Look at the following classification of the services offered by the International Trade division of Credit Bank International and complete the description below of how these services are organised.

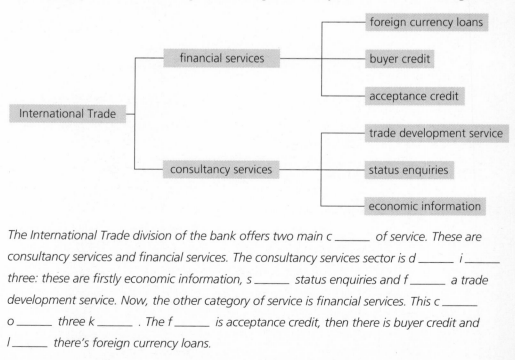

The International Trade division of the bank offers two main c _____ of service. These are consultancy services and financial services. The consultancy services sector is d _____ i _____ three: these are firstly economic information, s _____ status enquiries and f _____ a trade development service. Now, the other category of service is financial services. This c _____ o _____ three k _____ . The f _____ is acceptance credit, then there is buyer credit and l _____ there's foreign currency loans.

CLASSIFYING INFORMATION; CONNECTING and SEQUENCING IDEAS (2)

See LOBE:
Unit 73 – Classifying information
Unit 74 – Connecting and sequencing ideas

Exercise 1

Match the expression on the left with an expression on the right which means approximately the same.

1	subsequently	**a**	that is to say
2	sort	**b**	step
3	in other words	**c**	instead
4	consists of	**d**	splits into
5	stage	**e**	is made up of
6	above all	**f**	then
7	furthermore	**g**	most importantly
8	alternatively	**h**	in addition
9	divides into	**i**	type

Exercise 2

Look at the chart showing the product types offered by a major supermarket chain. Then complete the interview between a journalist and a store manager using words from the box.

consist	categories	included	divided	basic	comprises	under

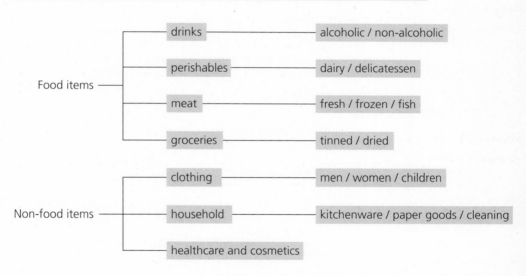

J: So, first of all, can you say how the products you sell are categorised?

M: Yes, it's quite simple. We have two basic product _____ , food and non-food items.

J: And what does each category _____ of?

M: Basically, food items _____ four classes: groceries, meat, perishables and drinks. And _____ non-food items we have healthcare and cosmetics, household goods and clothing.

J: What sort of things are _____ under household goods?

M: There are three _____ types: kitchenware, paper goods and cleaning materials. And then under perishables, we have dairy products and foods sold on the delicatessen. Meat is _____ into three kinds: fresh meat, frozen meat and fish.

UNIT 67

DESCRIBING the ORGANISATION

See LOBE:
Unit 76 – Describing the organisation

Exercise 1

Complete the organigram with words from the box.

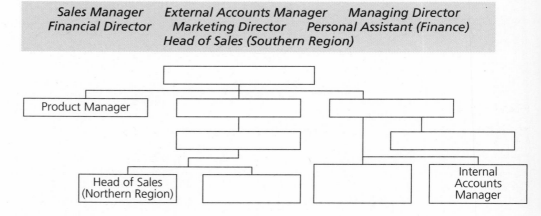

> Sales Manager   External Accounts Manager   Managing Director
> Financial Director   Marketing Director   Personal Assistant (Finance)
> Head of Sales (Southern Region)

Exercise 2

Which job title in the following groups of three is the 'odd one out'?

1 Managing Director	Sales Manager	Vice-President (Marketing)
2 Senior Vice-President	Chief Executive Officer	Company Director
3 Assistant Supervisor	Chargehand	Production Manager
4 Secretary	Personal Assistant	Human Resources Director

Exercise 3

Look at the following diagram which shows the organisation of a British University. Then complete the interview that follows, which is with the Director of Corporate Affairs. Use the appropriate form of words in the box.

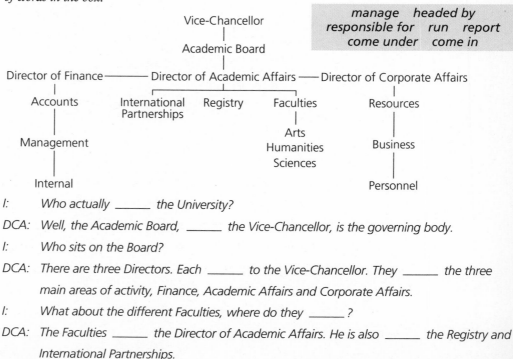

> manage   headed by
> responsible for   run   report
> come under   come in

I: Who actually _____ the University?

DCA: Well, the Academic Board, _____ the Vice-Chancellor, is the governing body.

I: Who sits on the Board?

DCA: There are three Directors. Each _____ to the Vice-Chancellor. They _____ the three
main areas of activity, Finance, Academic Affairs and Corporate Affairs.

I: What about the different Faculties, where do they _____ ?

DCA: The Faculties _____ the Director of Academic Affairs. He is also _____ the Registry and
International Partnerships.

See LOBE:
Unit 75 – Describing trends

Exercise 1

Which word in the following groups of four is the 'odd one out'?

1 rise	increase	climb	raise
2 expand	develop	shrink	grow
3 drop	fall	decline	peak
4 impressive	slight	substantial	considerable
5 dramatic	huge	sudden	slump
6 fluctuation	drop	reduction	collapse

Exercise 2

Match the following expressions to the appropriate graph below.

1 sudden fall	4 decline gradually
2 bottom out	5 marked fluctuation
3 remain constant	6 impressive rise

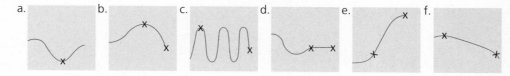

a.   b.   c.   d.   e.   f.

Exercise 3

Look at the graph below comparing sales of three products, A, B and C, over a five-year period. Complete the key to the graph and then complete the text using an appropriate form of the word in brackets.

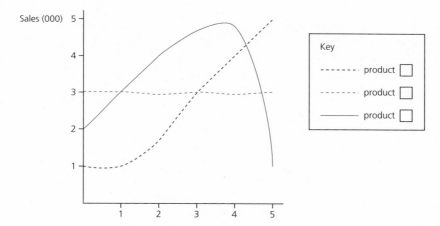

'We can see how differently the three products have performed. Firstly, Product A has shown a _____ (continue) climb in sales and now _____ (stand) at $5000 per year. In contrast, five years ago Product B had sales of over $3000 but since then has not _____ (increase). But the performance of Product B is still good, having more or less _____ _____ (remain constant) over the five-year period. Now, let's compare these with Product C which shows the most _____ (dramatically) trend, _____ (rise) from $2000 five years ago to reach a peak of almost $5000 in the fourth year before beginning a _____ (suddenly) decline to its present level of just $1000, a _____ (reduce) that is practically a complete _____ (collapsed).'

UNIT 69

COMPARING and CONTRASTING IDEAS

See LOBE:
Unit 79 – Contrasting ideas
Unit 80 – Comparing ideas

Exercise 1

Match the word or phrase on the left with a word or phrase on the right which means almost the same.

1	totally different from	a	practically the same as
2	despite	b	whereas
3	in comparison to	c	corresponds to
4	matches	d	in marked contrast to
5	very similar to	e	compared with
6	but	f	in spite of

Exercise 2

Look at the graph showing the trend in global water use over 100 years, comparing agricultural, industrial and municipal use. Complete this interview with a World Health Organisation official. Use words from the box.

> greater   in spite of   whereas
> even more   however   while

I: Can you describe the trend in world water use over the century?

O: Well, for 60 years, industrial and domestic use of water was insignificant, _____ agricultural use was relatively high even in 1900. _____ , suddenly there was a huge increase in domestic use and _____ for industrial use. _____ this, the real shock comes when we look at agricultural use. This is now up to three times _____ than industrial use and it is still increasing dramatically. _____ all three types of use are increasing, agricultural use is positively rocketing.

World water use: (cubic kilometres p.a.)

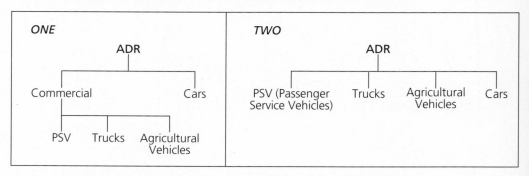

Exercise 3

Look at the two proposals for a new organisation of ADR Automotive Group. Rewrite each sentence that follows, keeping the same meaning, but using the word(s) in brackets.

ONE

ADR
Commercial   Cars
PSV   Trucks   Agricultural Vehicles

TWO

ADR
PSV (Passenger Service Vehicles)   Trucks   Agricultural Vehicles   Cars

1   Proposal 1 involves a Commercial Vehicle Division which, in terms of status, <u>matches</u> the Cars Division. (be/similar)
2   <u>Whereas</u> Proposal 2 <u>differs</u> in that Cars appears to <u>be no greater than</u> PSV or Agricultural Vehicles. (On the other hand/different/correspond)
3   In reality Cars accounts for 50 per cent of our business, so Proposal 1 <u>looks more like</u> the actual situation. (resemble/more closely)
4   <u>Despite</u> this objection, the Board prefers Proposal 2. (In spite of)

ASSERTING and DOWNTONING INFORMATION

See LOBE:
Unit 77 – Asserting and downtoning information

Exercise 1

Change the following phrases to the style indicated, using the words in brackets.

1   That's impossible.   Neutral   (not/think/possible)
2   I tend to think we can't do that.   Assertive   (sure/out of the question)
3   We can't expect to have an easy time.   Assertive   (clearly/will not)
4   The report says the product is useless.   Downtoning   (suggest/problems)

Exercise 2

Read the nine sentences below and mark them as A (assertive), N (neutral) or D (downtoning). Then reorganise them to make three different conversations, each containing only assertive, neutral or downtoning remarks.

1   Whatever we do, I'm inclined to think costs will limit our actions.
2   It's quite obvious that the test was badly designed.
3   Shall we ask the R & D team to send a representative?
4   I wonder if we ought to bring in some outside experts.
5   That's totally impossible – we spent three months planning it.
6   I think we should call another meeting.
7   It doesn't matter if you spent three years on it.
8   Yes, that's a good idea.
9   It might be a good idea to see if we have the money for that.

Exercise 3

Rephrase the totally inappropriate conversation below, downtoning each person's remarks. Keep the same basic meaning. Use the words in brackets.

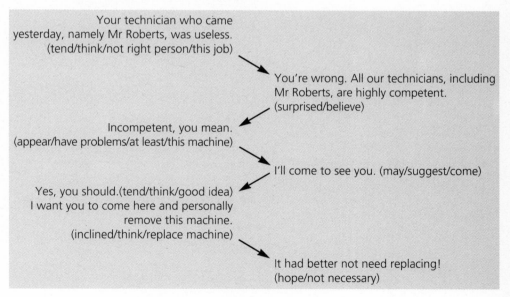

Your technician who came yesterday, namely Mr Roberts, was useless.
(tend/think/not right person/this job)

You're wrong. All our technicians, including Mr Roberts, are highly competent.
(surprised/believe)

Incompetent, you mean.
(appear/have problems/at least/this machine)

I'll come to see you. (may/suggest/come)

Yes, you should.(tend/think/good idea)
I want you to come here and personally remove this machine.
(inclined/think/replace machine)

It had better not need replacing!
(hope/not necessary)

UNIT 71

CHECKING and CONFIRMING INFORMATION

See LOBE:
Unit 81 – Checking and confirming information

Exercise 1

Use the flow chart below to create a telephone conversation in which a caller asks a computer help line for assistance.

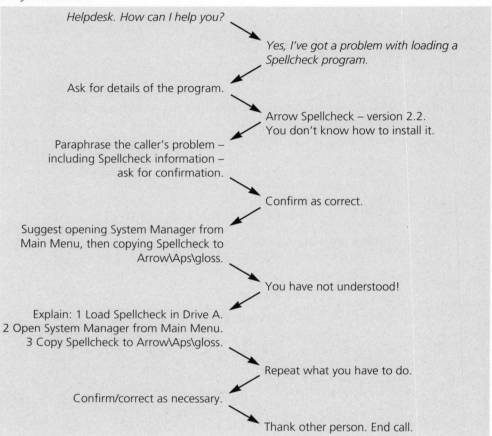

Helpdesk. How can I help you?

Yes, I've got a problem with loading a Spellcheck program.

Ask for details of the program.

Arrow Spellcheck – version 2.2. You don't know how to install it.

Paraphrase the caller's problem – including Spellcheck information – ask for confirmation.

Confirm as correct.

Suggest opening System Manager from Main Menu, then copying Spellcheck to Arrow\Aps\gloss.

You have not understood!

Explain: 1 Load Spellcheck in Drive A.
2 Open System Manager from Main Menu.
3 Copy Spellcheck to Arrow\Aps\gloss.

Repeat what you have to do.

Confirm/correct as necessary.

Thank other person. End call.

Exercise 2

Below is part of an interview with an economist about prospects for economic recovery in the UK. Fill in the spaces using phrases from the box.

> **explain in more detail   as I've already said   are you saying
> in other words   to paraphrase what you've said**

E: An unfavourable labour market is threatening the prospects for economic recovery in many sectors of the economy.

J: Could you _____ what that means?

E: Well, labour costs and a highly regulated employment market make unit labour costs much higher than in competitor economies.

J: _____ wages are too high?

E: Certainly that's true. But other factors contribute to labour costs, such as insurance costs, equal pay laws, restrictive working practices, health and safety conditions.

J: So, _____ a whole range of social legislation is responsible for labour costs.

E: Yes. All this, _____, makes labour very expensive.

J: So, _____, high labour costs and a restrictive labour market are damaging the prospects for recovery?

E: That's it. I believe so.

See LOBE:
Unit 82 – Likes and preferences

Exercise 1

Thomas and Maria have to arrange a meeting. Rewrite the underlined phrases using the words in brackets. Do not change the original meaning.

T: Can we fix a meeting soon?

M: Yes, when <u>do you want to meet</u>? (like/meet)

T: <u>I think</u> early next month. (rather/be)

M: Hmm. I think that should be okay, but <u>it would be better for me on</u> a Monday. (prefer)

T: That's no problem. Now, where? Where<u>'s best for you</u>? Your office or mine? (prefer)

M: <u>If possible</u>, in a beautiful holiday resort, Bermuda for example! (rather/meet)

T: Yes, Bermuda's great. But <u>my choice is</u> your office. (like/come) <u>You have better</u> coffee. (prefer) Also, I <u>always enjoy going</u> to that French restaurant round the corner. (like/go)

Exercise 2

Annette and Paula meet when travelling abroad. Here they are discussing business trips. Underline and then correct any mistakes.

A: Where do you usually stay, in a family-run hotel or in a big chain hotel like this one?

P: I prefer stay in a big chain hotel, because when I'm on business I only think about work. When I travel with my family, then I am liking a more personal hotel.

A: So you don't go out to the theatre or enjoy yourself when you're on business?

P: Actually, I rarely go to the theatre. I like more music, so I go to concerts.

A: Yes, so do I. Do you like go to a concert this evening?

P: I like that, but unfortunately I have a meeting this evening. But what's the concert?

A: It's an evening of Mozart at the City Hall.

P: That would be good, but I have to say I prefer more Beethoven.

A: I think I do too. Let me get you a drink. What do you like?

P: I'd like that I have an apple juice.

Exercise 3

Choose the correct alternative to complete the sentences below.

A: Would you like/rather to see a copy of the report before the meeting?

B: Yes, I'd prefer/like to see/seeing it as soon as possible.

A: Do you want/like me to come to the meeting?

B: I'd prefer/like you didn't come.

A: That's fine. I'd rather/like stay away.

UNIT 73

LIKES and PREFERENCES; ASKING FOR and GIVING OPINIONS

See LOBE:
Unit 82 – Likes and preferences
Unit 83 – Asking for and giving opinions

Exercise 1

Two colleagues are discussing the relocation of their plant to a country area, away from its present city location. Create a dialogue based on the flow chart below.

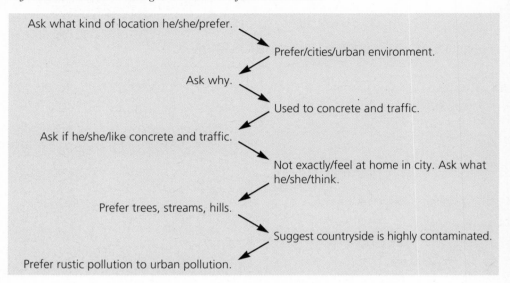

Ask what kind of location he/she/prefer.

Prefer/cities/urban environment.

Ask why.

Used to concrete and traffic.

Ask if he/she/like concrete and traffic.

Not exactly/feel at home in city. Ask what he/she/think.

Prefer trees, streams, hills.

Suggest countryside is highly contaminated.

Prefer rustic pollution to urban pollution.

Exercise 2

Change the following strongly expressed opinions to more moderately expressed opinions.

1 The rural location will definitely mean higher transport costs.
2 Relocation will obviously create domestic problems for our staff.
3 Clearly a lot of people will work from home.
4 Working from home also creates domestic problems, I'm sure.
5 There's no point in moving – the costs will be enormous.

Exercise 3

Put an adverb or adverbial phrase in the following sentences to make them stronger.

1 We should reconsider the decision.
2 We cannot do this without everyone's support.
3 There is a danger that we have chosen the wrong location.
4 We have to look at all the drawbacks again.
5 The decision to move is in the best interests of the company.

ASKING FOR and GIVING OPINIONS; AGREEING and DISAGREEING (1)

See LOBE:
Unit 83 – Asking for and giving opinions
Unit 84 – Agreeing and disagreeing

Exercise 1

Complete the following phrases with suitable words.

A: So I'd _____ _____ ask you what you _____ about this research problem.
B: My _____ is that we _____ take on a new Research Officer.
A: You _____ be right, _____ we have to think about the costs.
C: I'm sorry, I _____ _____ with Ben. I _____ think we already have enough people in Research.

Exercise 2

The Managing Director of Logicam has invited the Marketing Manager to discuss communication processes in the company. Read the following extract from their conversation, and underline:

1 an example of asking for opinion *indirectly*
2 two examples of asking for opinion *directly* (there are three)
3 an example of a strongly held opinion
4 two examples of weakly expressed opinion
5 three examples of expressing agreement
6 one example of disagreement

MD: So, I'm concerned about the quality of communication here in Logicam. I was wondering what your views might be on how we operate, in the area of communication processes. You've no doubt got a lot of experience in this…

MM: Well, I'm not sure I have a lot, I've only been here six months…

MD: … but you have expertise and experience in other companies and, more importantly, you see Logicam with fresh eyes. What do you think of communication here?

MM: Well, I'm sure it could be improved and I know people complain … you know, too much paper, poor use of IT …

MD: So, do you have any suggestions? How can we improve things?

MM: Well, first of all I think I'd recommend a communications audit, you know, an assessment of the situation, find out what happens, what people think.

MD: Yes, I'm sure you're right. I was thinking along those lines. Could you do that?

MM: Well, no, I don't have much expertise in this area, but also, I think it would be better if we used an outsider, someone independent, not directly involved.

MD: Yes, I can see the advantages there. So, a consultant then?

MM: Yes, but they'd need to get to know us. Or a combination, someone from inside the company, together with a consultant.

MD: That might be possible, a possible way. So, you think it could be effective, like that?

MM: I think it could be, but I'm inclined to think it would be a long process. Getting to know the company, making proposals, having discussions, making recommendations, implementing decisions, auditing the results of implementation … so, a long project.

MD: Do you have anyone in mind?

MM: Yes, as it happens, my husband is a Communications Consultant …

See LOBE:
Unit 83 – Asking for and giving opinions
Unit 84 – Agreeing and disagreeing

Exercise 1

Agree with the following statements (a) strongly, then (b) weakly.

1 The problem is one of size. We're too small.
2 We need to be more ambitious, to do bigger things.
3 But I am concerned that we don't have the resources.

Exercise 2

Disagree with the following statements (a) strongly, then (b) weakly.

1 We would never win the contract with Acos Ltd.
2 We can't compete with Gubu.
3 Mr Roach is the best man for the job.

Exercise 3

Complete the following mini-dialogues with appropriate words.

A: So, what _____ you _____ about the Hurst plan?

B: I'm _____ to think it won't work.

A: Really? Surely you are being pessimistic?

B: I think we'd have problems.

A: What _____ of problems?

A: The weakness in the plan is that it is not properly costed.

B: I'm sorry, I can't _____ that. We costed every detail.

C: Yes, I think we did, but the costs are too high.

B: Yes, they are high, _____ on the other hand, I don't think we have any choice.

A: Henry thinks the insurance costs are too high.

H: No, I _____ say that. I simply said they **are** high.

B: Well, Henry, I don't think I _____ agree _____ you. In fact, they're reasonable.

A: Can I _____ if anyone has any views on the price? Ben?

B: I _____ to think it's okay.

C: Yes, it's okay, but I also think we _____ look at alternatives.

D: We've spent enough time on this already. We should go ahead.

C: No. We have to get it right.

A: This is a brilliant idea!

B: No it _____ . It'll _____ work.

A: You're _____ . You'll see.

Exercise 1

Rewrite the following sentences using the correct form of the word given in brackets and adding any other necessary words. The first has been done as an example.

1   The continued hot and dry weather has caused a water shortage. (result)
    The continued hot and dry weather has resulted in a water shortage.
2   The shortage has resulted in a government decision to introduce restrictions on water. (lead)
3   The restrictions may be responsible for some financial savings. (bring)
4   Abuse of the restrictions may result in prosecutions. (give rise)
5   In some areas, the restrictions on water use lead to problems for industry. (cause)

Exercise 2

Here is an extract from a newspaper about the effects of tourism. Underline causes with a straight line and effects with a wavy line. Then complete the brief memo summarising cause and effect relationships in the second paragraph of the report.

Damage to monuments

The city authority is concerned about the effect on the infrastructure of the city of large and increasing volumes of tourists. A recent report claims that high volume tourism is changing the character of the city centre.

Many businesses have moved away from the town centre because local people no longer enjoy shopping there. Also, the volume of visitors has resulted in damage to some historic monuments. For example, large numbers of visitors have affected some of the 700-year-old paintings in the Cathedral. In another example, coachloads of visitors to Liberation Park have resulted in a reduction in some species of bird life on the ponds.

MEMO

Subject: Growth in tourism
To: SS   *From:* IFT   *Date:* 21. 9. 96

Businesses _____ local people _____ .
The volume of visitors _____ monuments.
Large numbers of visitors _____ paintings in Cathedral.
Coachloads of visitors to the park _____ birds.

Exercise 3

At a public enquiry into the sinking of a passenger ferry, a journalist made the following notes on the conclusions of the enquiry. Write five sentences containing cause and effect relationships. Use the words in brackets to link cause and effect.

1 *ship sank –*
   water entering lower car deck   (due to)
2 *water entering lower car deck –*
   insecure bow door   (as a consequence of)
3 *door not closed properly –*
   poor working practices   (because of)
4 *frequently careless work –*
   inadequate supervision   (owing to)
5 *commercial pressures –*
   unreasonable hurry to leave port area   (attributable to)

See LOBE:
Unit 85 – Cause and effect
Unit 86 – Obligations and requirements

Exercise 1

The text below is part of the instructions for using an automatic warehousing platform. The diagram shows the control panel. Read the text, then create a conversation based on the flow chart, in which a representative of the manufacturer, Alfonsin S.A., is explaining to an agent how the machine works.

Notes: (+) = obligation to do something
(–) = no obligation to do something
(–0) = obligation not to do something.

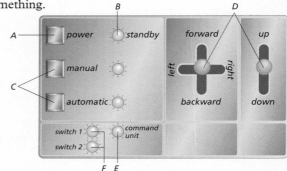

Operating Instructions

1 Switch on power (A).
2 Stand-by light (B) should illuminate. If it does not, check switches 1 and 2 on base unit (F).
3 Select manual or automatic (C). If you choose automatic, the panel controls (D) are deactivated. The platform will operate totally automatically.
4 If you choose manual, the platform must be operated using the panel controls (D).
5 If the stand-by light (B) is illuminated and the platform is switched to manual but the pane controls (D) do not work, inspect the electronic command unit (ECU) on base unit.
6 If the command unit light (E) is illuminated, inspect the ECU.
7 If the switch 1 or 2 lights (F) are illuminated, change fuse in the switches on base unit.
8 Do not attempt to carry out ECU repairs. Contact your local agent.

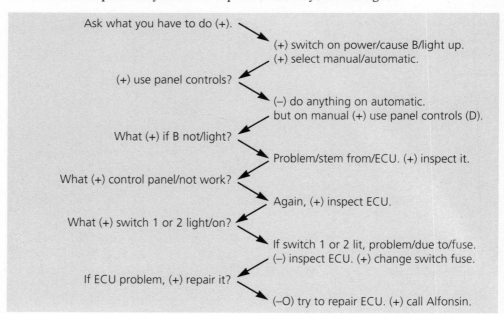

Exercise 2

*Look at the control panel in the diagram above. Write three cause and effect sentences about the movement of the platform. Use the following verbs: **make, cause, result in.***

Example:

See LOBE:
Unit 86 – Obligations and requirements

Exercise 1

Here is part of a letter from the Head Office of a bank to branches. It is about new restrictions on providing financial services for customers. Fill in the correct form of the verbs from the box.

require   ban   need   permit   suppose   oblige   force

Credit Bank International

22-28 Wellington Row
LONDON W1R 7RT

12 May 19…

Dear Colleagues,
With reference to recent legislation affecting financial service organisations, I am writing with some guidelines to help you adapt to the changes.

All financial service advisors, banks and building societies are now _____ by law to write to individual clients setting out the terms of their engagements. The new regulations _____ companies to give detailed descriptions of the work they are qualified to do. They are also _____ to specify all charges and commissions.

A further change is that all individuals working as advisors _____ to be fully qualified. Anyone without the necessary professional qualifications is _____ from giving financial advice. As a result many individuals with years of experience will be _____ to take professional examinations. Unqualified persons will no longer be _____ to give even informal advice.

I am sure that given our consistently high standards, we will not have any difficulty in conforming to the new legislation. Meanwhile, do contact me in the event of any concern.

Yours sincerely,

Robert Bigg

Director of Corporate Services

Exercise 2

The text below is part of a fax from an architect to a manager of a company planning to build new offices. Complete the table which follows with the numbers of the points.

From: Maiko Kusuyama (Art Grant Associates)
Our fax: 01482 454561 Telephone: 01482 454700

FAX MESSAGE
For attention of: James Zillessen
Re. Maple Project: Your letter/planning regulations

1 Access to all public areas must include provision for wheelchairs.
2 The regulations oblige us to provide toilet facilities for the disabled.
3 We are not compelled to have a fire door on the long corridor.
4 We are prohibited from installing windows in the east facing wall.
5 We do not need to have a sky light over the rear stairs.
6 We are supposed to guarantee adequate lighting for all areas.

Obligation	No obligation	Obligation not to do something

See LOBE:
Unit 86 – Obligations and requirements
Unit 87 – Ability and inability

Exercise 1

Re-write the underlined parts of the following sentences using the words in brackets.

1 Due to management ruling, <u>we can no longer use Room 4.</u> (use of/banned)
2 We regret this machine <u>is unable to provide</u> all the goods you require. (not capable)
3 <u>There are restrictions on</u> the amount of electricity we may use. (restricted)
4 We <u>are unable to offer you</u> the credit facilities we have made available to you in the past. (forced/withdraw)
5 <u>It is not necessary for you to</u> visit next week. (need)
6 We <u>must</u> make major cost savings. (compelled)

Exercise 2

Complete the fax below using words from the box.

| be able | banned | prohibited | unable | can | allowed | permitted |

GUBU TOYS (EIRE) LIMITED

FAX to Sales and Distribution
Attention: Shona J. Keele
Fax: 221 - 987443

From: Gubu Toys Ltd
West Drive Industrial Park
Dublin 22 EIRE
FAX: 353-1-467500
Phone: 353-1-322800

Please delay despatch of our order number TR/09/4577.

The import of certain products which we have in the past obtained from you is no longer _____ since the introduction of tougher safety controls. I will send you a full list of the regulations as they affect your products.

In the meantime please note that we have stocks of certain products that we are _____ to sell. Please tell us if you _____ take back these items. You may _____ _____ to modify them.

Please note the following:

1 attachments of the type used on TR396 are now _____ .

2 we are _____ from selling existing stock of TR431

3 we are not _____ to sell TR397 on account of the metal ring.

We await your response to this information.

Regards,

Cathy Synge

Marketing Director

CAUSE and EFFECT; ABILITY and INABILITY

See LOBE:
Unit 85 – Cause and effect
Unit 87 – Ability and inability

Exercise 1

The following phrases are extracts from an article on the world market for musical instruments.
Match the phrase on the left to an appropriate ending on the right.

1 High-quality products and good management	**a** American manufacturers have been unable to rely on their traditional markets.
2 Importers of Japanese musical instruments	**b** other manufacturers cannot beat them in this important respect.
3 Low unit costs in Japan	**c** are able to find enthusiastic agents throughout Europe.
4 Since the tonality of the Japanese instruments is so good,	**d** have led to a powerful world market position.
5 As a result of the increasing strength of the Japanese musical instruments industry,	**e** permit manufacturers to keep costs down.

Exercise 2

Read the following extract from an article on surgical techniques in a health magazine, and identify:

1 six consequences of non-invasive surgery
2 what non-invasive surgery permits the surgeon to do
3 what makes it possible for the surgeon to see inside the body
4 what allows delicate operations with little damage to healthy tissue

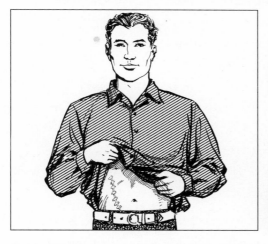

Non-invasive surgery using fibre optic technology and laser beams has resulted in considerable improvements in treatment for a range of conditions. One of the many benefits resulting from these developments has been the lower risk of infection and improved healing times. Patients are therefore able to leave hospital relatively quickly. This has also brought about considerable cost benefits and enabled more patients to be treated more quickly.

Non-invasive surgery means the surgeon can perform operations on internal organs without having to make major incisions. Optical fibre and laser equipment, linked to a monitor, allows the surgeon to see a magnified image of the target tissue in the body. Sophisticated control mechanisms permit delicate operations to be performed with minimum damage to surrounding tissue.

Now look at the text again and identify:

5 four words or phrases indicating cause and effect
6 four words indicating ability

UNIT 81

ABILITY and INABILITY; SCALE OF LIKELIHOOD

See LOBE:
Unit 87 – Ability and inability
Unit 88 – Scale of likelihood

Exercise 1

Match the phrase on the left with one on the right which means almost the same.

1	ban something	a	prevent (someone doing) something
2	be allowed (to do something)	b	be unable to manage something
3	be able (to do something)	c	be permitted (to do something)
4	stop (someone doing) something	d	prohibit something
5	be incapable (of doing something)	e	be in a position to do something

Exercise 2

Complete the following paragraph with words from the box.

incapable   bound   likely   unable   prevented

It is quite _____ that the world air travel market will see major changes in the near future. There is a problem of over-capacity, with many airlines _____ of increasing their market share. Smaller airlines are already largely prevented from operating on the most popular routes. There are _____ to be more takeovers, as smaller airlines prove _____ to compete.

Exercise 3

Here is an extract from a speech made by Dan Cavan, Chairman of Credit Bank International, at the company Annual General Meeting. He is talking about a failed acquisition attempt.

'Last year I said that it was very probable that during the year we would increase our market share by buying up a smaller competitor. It's no secret that we hoped to join up with Northern Bank. Despite strenuous efforts, we weren't capable of persuading the Northern Bank shareholders that our offer was a good one for them. Naturally, as a result of shareholder opposition, the board of Northern wasn't allowed to continue talks with us. So the merger couldn't go ahead. Despite this disappointment, we feel that we may now be capable of an improved offer for Northern next year. I would estimate that it's quite probable that the merger will eventually happen. On the other hand, other rival banks have expressed an interest. There's nothing to stop them attempting to take over Northern. Indeed, I expect them to try.'

Here is part of a newspaper report on the speech. Fill in the spaces, using different words from those used by the Chairman above.

Bank takeover battle predicted

Dan Cavan, Chairman of Credit Bank International, said yesterday at the CBI Annual General Meeting, that it is almost _____ that other banks, as well as his own, will try to take over Northern Bank. He claimed that last year the takeover of Northern Bank by CBI was considered _____ _____ . However, CBI was _____ to persuade NB shareholders to accept the merger. Indeed, the NB board was _____ _____ continuing talks. He went on to say that now CBI may be in a _____ to make a better offer for Northern.

86

SCALE OF LIKELIHOOD

See LOBE:
Unit 88 – Scale of likelihood

Exercise 1

Look at the diagram below which represents the scale of likelihood of five things happening to a United States Pipeline manufacturer, Petersburg Pipeline Systems Inc., in the coming year. Write a sentence for each possibility, indicating the degree of likelihood. The first is done as an example.

It is absolutely impossible that the company will be taken over by a competitor.

    0 ┌─ Be taken over by a competitor
   25 ├─ Increase stake in European associate companies
   50 ├─ Improve existing 14 per cent global market share
   75 ├─ Achieve record sales of TriValve system
  100 └─ Open new production plant in Seoul

Exercise 2

Each of the following sentences is in some way illogical. Correct them.

1 Given that he is very clever, it is unlikely that he will be successful.
2 I am certain that she might be the best person to lead the team.
3 I'm a little bit certain that she will accept the appointment.
4 It is improbable that we'll be successful so I'm bound to be optimistic.
5 We may be bound to benefit from increased publicity.

Exercise 3

At a board meeting of a soft drinks manufacturer, the Marketing Director talks about the company's sponsorship of a football team. Match the situation described on the left with a corresponding description of likelihood on the right. The first has been done as an example.

1	The club have won two cups this year.	a	They are bound to feature on television a lot in the coming year.
2	We have benefited from sponsoring the football team for the past three years.	b	It is quite likely that they will win a major competition again next year.
3	They enjoy a very high profile, being frequently on television.	c	It is highly probable that consumers will continue to associate our name with this lifestyle.
4	Our association with sport is good for our youthful and healthy image.	d	I feel sure that we will reach an agreement to extend our deal by a further three years.

UNIT ◆83◆

ADVISING and SUGGESTING

See LOBE:
Unit 89 – Advising and suggesting

Exercise 1

Complete the following sentences.

1 Why _____ you call your agent?

2 I think you _____ speak to him as soon as possible.

3 I suggest _____ find out what the problem is.

4 We _____ to have a decision on what to do.

5 If we can't decide, I _____ having another meeting next week.

6 No, _____ solve the problem today.

7 How _____ having a short break?

Exercise 2

During a meeting to discuss the breach of a contract by a supplier, Arco Metal, the following suggestions were made.

John Smith: We ought to get our Legal Department to examine exactly how they are

                              breaking the terms of the contract.

Carla Viraggio: We should ask Arco for a meeting to discuss ways to resolve the problem.

Tom Henson: I think you should get independent legal advice.

Meeting conclusion: No decision yet. Meet again Monday.

Complete the note below to a colleague who missed the meeting because of a trip abroad. Report the three suggestions and the conclusion. Use the verbs from the box.

recommend	suggest	advise	agree

CONFIDENTIAL MEMORANDUM

```
To: HF
From:JS
Re. Arco Metal - Contract dispute

Since you will be away for a few more days, I thought I would
give you an update on the above problem.
At a recent meeting, three suggestions were made:
John Smith _____
Carla V. _____
Finally, Tom H. _____
In conclusion, it _____
Look forward to hearing your views!

Best wishes,
```

Exercise 3

You are a Section Manager in a large Australian manufacturing company. One of your colleagues, Brigitte, has a personnel problem with two members of her staff, Sam and Paul, who do not get on well together. Write an informal letter, suggesting certain actions. Make the points listed below, using the words in brackets.

1 Relocate one of the two (Paul) to a different office. (recommend)
2 Eliminate the possibility of Paul having to take orders from Sam. (suggest)
3 Ask Personnel to move one of them to another department. (should)
4 Have a meeting with them to get them to change their attitude to one another. (why not)

REQUESTING INFORMATION and ACTION

See LOBE:
Unit 90 – Requesting information and action

Exercise 1

Identify which of the following sentences ask for information (I) and which ask for action (A).
Identify the two most direct forms (D) and the two most indirect forms (IND).

1 I would be grateful if you could send me some samples of your recent work.
2 Please send them to my colleague in New York, Barbara Svensson.
3 It would help me if you could let me know the range of typefaces you normally use in printing the publicity material.
4 Could you please write to Ms Svensson telling her about the Quality Circle meeting.
5 We need to know the names of anyone coming next week, to book accommodation.

Exercise 2

Write a dialogue between a customer requiring catering supplies and a food wholesaler.

Q: Ask if they have 100 2 kg packs of cheese and basil tortellini.	A: Say there is no problem.
Q: Ask them if they could despatch them this morning for delivery later today.	A: Suggest order is made by fax.
Q: Agree. Ask for 20 l. of Spanish olive oil.	A: Agree.
Q: Ask what time delivery will arrive.	A: Offer to call back to say.
Q: Ask supplier to find out in the next 10 minutes.	A: Agree.

Exercise 3

The following is part of a report from a paper manufacturer, Papeleras Pascual, on some production difficulties. In a later conversation, the Production Manager is asking a colleague to take certain actions, based on the recommendations in the report. Match the phrase on the left with an appropriate ending on the right. The first is done for you as an example.

Papeleras Pascual S.A. Tolosa, Guipuzcoa, SPAIN
Production Report

Date: 12 May 19…
Subject: Paper production quality

Observations
1 There has been some variation in colour using GD342 dye. This dye, rarely used, is an important ingredient in achieving colours in the range K21-26.
2 The printing has shown poor definition – probably a heat problem.
3 We are very low on stocks of ethylene cleaning agent.
4 The samples selected are not enough to give a total picture of roll quality.
5 Occasional tearing at end of roll.
6 Variation in gauge (thickness) in two recent orders, J4521 and J4587, has been noted.

Recommendations
a Contact supplier: ask them to check paper weight and consistent gauge.
b Check temperature controls.

1 I think we ought to
2 Then I recommend
3 But also, would you please
4 You should have
5 I suggest that

a you make an immediate order for 100 litres of ethylene 200.
b the blade sharpened.
c check the temperature controls.
d carrying out stability tests on the dye.
e take samples at shorter intervals.

PART 3

KEY

UNIT 1

Exercise 1

1 Right.
2 Wrong. I **work** for ABC in the accounts department.
3 Right.
4 Wrong. At present we **are launching** a new market campaign.
5 Wrong. The company **is starting** to export to other countries.
6 Right.
7 Wrong. Our future **depends** on the new financial team.

Exercise 2

Richard: How **do** you **do**? My name **is** Richard Li.
Isabel: Pleased to meet you. I **am** Isabel de Miguel.
Richard: So, where **do** you **come** from?
Isabel: From Spain. I **work** in the Madrid office.
Richard: So, I **suppose** that you **are working** on the new IT project.
Isabel: That's right. But how **do** you **know** about the project? We **are trying** to keep it confidential.
Richard: Yes, I **know.** But we **belong** to the same project team. In fact we **are carrying out** the same trials at the moment.
Isabel: Really. Well, how many people **does** your project **involve**?
Richard: I'm afraid I **don't know**. In fact no-one **knows**. It's confidential at the moment!

Exercise 3

Good morning, ladies and gentlemen. My name **is** Gilles Latour. I **work** in the marketing department as a product manager. In this short presentation I **intend** to cover three main points. Firstly, the company's major activities; secondly, our present product range; and finally our future plans. If you **have** any questions, please **don't hesitate** to ask.
As you **know**, we **specialise** in customised software. Our clients **include** major corporations on both sides of the Atlantic. We typically **divide** our activities into control systems and multimedia applications. At present the market for the latter **is increasing** substantially. And for the former, we **don't expect** to see an increase in the near future. We **employ** some 250 people at our site in Newtown. And currently we **are looking for** engineers for a new project for a Central European client. In addition to the permanent workforce, the company regularly **uses** consultants at the customers' sites. They **help** us in areas such as installation and testing. OK, that **covers** the first point. Now **let**'s move on to the products in more detail.

UNIT 2

Exercise 1

| 1 | d | 2 | e | 3 | b |
| 4 | c | 5 | a | | |

Exercise 2

I **wrote** to you at this time last year to inform you of the developments in our company. At that time, we **were negotiating** with the French company Hypervend for a share of the supermarket business. Hypervend subsequently **accepted** our proposal and our products **started** to appear on the shelves at the end of the year. However, some six months later we **found** that customers **were buying** more and more rival French products. Hypervend's management **said** that we **weren't packaging** our products for French consumers, who **were moving** to lighter and more colourful designs. We therefore **asked** you to study French packaging tastes. As I **said** when you **completed** your study, we **felt** that your approach **didn't get** to the heart of the matter.
Therefore, when we **received** your invoice, I was surprised to see....

Exercise 3

Interviewer: So how long **did** you **work** for Matthews?
David: Just over two years.
Interviewer: And what tests **did** you **carry out** while you **were working** there?
David: I first **investigated** their motivation problems.
Interviewer: And what **did** the results **show**?
David: In fact, while we **were processing** the results, the company **decided** to stop the project. You see, at the same time, the company **was/were developing** a new working model. And they **needed** additional people to implement that programme.
Interviewer: I see. So **did** you **move** on to that project?
David: Yes. But while we **were working** on that project, the European funds **stopped**. So, that's when I **decided** to leave.

UNIT 3

Exercise 1

1 Right.
2 Wrong. Since when **have you been working/have you worked** for ABC?
3 Right.
4 Wrong. I have been working for ABC **for** five years.
5 Wrong. Last year we ( ) introduced a new accounting system.
6 Right.
7 Wrong. I have **been writing** this report all morning.
8 Right in AmE.
  Wrong in BrE. I'm afraid Mr Davison isn't in his office. He **has** just **gone** out.

Exercise 2

Good morning, ladies and gentlemen. My name is Martin Winkler and I **work** in the R&D department here at Brymore. **I have been working** on this current project for two years now. The project team **consists** of myself and five engineers. Steven Brookes

has been with us since the start of the project and he **has developed** the prototype which you'll see later. At present we **are testing** the capacity of the prototype and we **expect** to have some results later this month.

Now on to the presentation itself. I **have divided** it into three parts which **I've written** up here on this transparency. The first part **covers** the project brief. The second part **deals** with the team, who **have brought** special knowledge and skills to the project. And the third part **looks** at the project stages. As you'll see, other companies and institutes **have been helping/have helped** us and we are very grateful for their assistance.

Exercise 3

1 c	**2** f	**3** d	**4** a
5 g	**6** b	**7** e	

UNIT 4

Exercise 1

1 Before we started building, we had to apply for planning permission.
2 While we were building the hotel, the planning regulations changed.
3 We explained that we had completed all the formalities.
4 The authorities said we hadn't followed the correct procedures.
5 While we were waiting for permission, one of our suppliers went bankrupt.
6 After they had gone bankrupt, we tried to find an alternative.

Exercise 2

Jo: So what **did** you **have to** do before you **started** the project?
Sarah: After we **received/had received** the funding, we **needed** to prepare a detailed specification.
Jo: How long **did** that **take**?
Sarah: Not long. After we **assembled/had assembled** the team, each member **worked** on their own part.
Jo: I see. And what **was happening** while everyone **was preparing** the specification?
Sarah: Nothing on this project. But everyone **continued** to work on their other projects until everything **was** ready. So, exactly three months after we **received/had received** the funding, we **began** the investigation.
Jo: So when **did** the problems **start**?
Sarah: One day, while we **were checking** the equipment, we **realised** that the computer **had not calculated** the right results since the beginning of the project.
Jo: I see. And do you know why the computer **was not working/did not work** properly?
Sarah: Not yet.

Exercise 3

1 c	**2** e	**3** a	
4 d	**5** b		

UNIT 5

Exercise 1

1 Right.
2 Wrong. I ( ) work in the Accounts Department.
3 Wrong. And how long **have you worked/have you been working** there?
4 Wrong. I ( ) joined the company eight years ago.
5 Right.
6 Wrong. I **have worked/have been working** there **for** four years.

Exercise 2

1 I am glad to report that sales **are increasing** at present.
2 I really **don't /didn't understand** these figures. What **do** they **mean**?
3 Last year we **reduced** the workforce by 8 percent.
4 At this time last year we **were enjoying/enjoyed** a big rise in sales.
5 **Have** you **read** this report on rationalisation yet? (Br E) Did you read this report on rationalisation yet? (Am E)
6 We **have been using/have used** our present consultants for three years now.
7 The MD reported that the company **had had** good results in the previous quarter.

Exercise 3

Paul: How **do** you **do**? My name **is** Paul Roberts.
Andreas: Pleased to meet you. Mine's Andreas Schmidt.
Paul: I **don't think** we **have met** before.
Andreas: No, I only **joined** the European firm nine months ago. Before that I **was working/worked** out in Bangkok.
Paul: What **were** you **doing/did** you **do** out there?
Andreas: I **managed** recruitment and selection for the South East Asian region. But then my wife **said** that she **had not seen** Europe for many years and that she **wanted** to go back.
Paul: And **did** you **agree**?
Andreas: Yes, of course. And **are** you **based** here in London?
Paul: No, actually I **work** in Madrid, though I **have lived/have been living** near London for many, many years. You **see** I **joined** the Spanish office when I **started** my career.
Andreas: But **doesn't** your family **mind** you working away from home?
Paul: Well, actually my wife **did**.
Andreas: So what **happened**?
Paul: Oh, we **got** divorced some time ago.

UNIT 6

Exercise 1 (M)

Don: When **does** the next training programme **start**?
Bill: We **are running** the next one in January.
Don: And how many participants **are going to attend**?
Bill: I expect that we **will have** at least twenty.
Don: **Are** you **going to arrange** an evening programme?
Bill: Probably, yes, but in any case we **are going to review** the arrangements before the seminar. **I'll send** you a copy of the programme, if you are interested.
Don: Thanks. When **will** the programme **be** ready?
Bill: By the end of next month.

Exercise 2

1	e	2	h	3	c	4	g
5	a	6	f	7	b	8	d

Exercise 3 (M)

Johan: So when **are** you **launching** the new product?
Henry: It's scheduled for next month, but we **are going to have to** make some changes.
Johan: And what about sales training?
Henry: We **are running** a series of workshops over the next two weeks.
Johan: Good. Look, Henry, I **am visiting** London next week. I'd like to come over and visit you.
Henry: When exactly **are** you **going to be** in London?
Johan: My plane **arrives** on Thursday at 2 o'clock.
Henry: Thursday afternoon's no good for me. What **are** you **doing** in the evening?
Johan: Nothing. I think **I'll book** a table for us at the Brasserie. About 8?
Henry: Sounds great. See you there.

UNIT 7

Exercise 1

1 Right.
2 Wrong. Provided we ( ) remain profitable, we can invest in our plant.
3 Right.
4 Wrong. If we **asked** for a bank loan tomorrow, I'm sure we would get it.
5 Right.
6 Right.
7 Wrong. If the economy **remained** stable, it would help industry.
8 Wrong. If we **had known** the scale of inflation, we could have reduced our running costs.

Exercise 2

1	c	2	f	3	a
4	e	5	b	6	d

Exercise 3

Chris: If we **want** to recruit better workers, we need to offer better rates of pay.
Maria: I disagree. Just look at Mansell. If we **had followed** their example, we **would be/would have been** bankrupt by now. If we **offer/offered** the highest wages, I doubt that it would make us a better employer.
Chris: Well, look at it the other way round. If we don't attract better workers, we simply **won't get** the orders.
Maria: Why not?
Chris: Because of investment. If a company **wants** to succeed it must invest in all aspects of the business. And that includes the workforce.
Maria: So, if we were to invest in the workforce, how **would** you **suggest** going about it?
Chris: I **would recommend** a study of the average wage in this area for different types of work. And then we should offer a competitive rate for different grades, as long as everyone **agreed**.
Maria: And what if they **didn't agree**?
Chris: Then Bob **would have to** make the final decision.

UNIT 8

Exercise 1

1	III	2	I	3	II

Exercise 2 (M)

1 If a customer is dissatisfied with the goods, s/he may return them within 28 days and claim a full refund.
2 Should a purchaser return the goods, all costs incurred in returning them shall be paid by the purchaser.
3 Goods will be accepted as long as they are returned in the original packaging and in full working order.
4 In the event that the company incurs any costs to prepare the goods for resale, these shall be deducted from the money to be repaid to the purchaser.
5 In case of any dispute under this contract, it shall first be presented at a commercial court.
6 Should a claimant wish to appeal against the decision of the commercial court, appeal may be made to a court of law.
7 The company shall not pay any costs in settling the dispute in any court unless the company has been negligent.

Exercise 3

1 In the event of a claim for injury, we will investigate it.
2 We can't carry out a full investigation unless we have all the documentation.
3 Should we require an external assessment, we will consult an expert.
4 In case you need the information, take a photocopy.
5 We will review your case, so long as you agree to bear any additional costs.

6 Were we to change our decision, we would reimburse all additional costs.
7 Provided that all papers have been received, we will settle all claims within 30 days.
8 Had you made a fraudulent claim, we would have taken you to court.

UNIT 9

Exercise 1

1 Right.
2 Wrong to describe normal job. I **work** for Manpower in the Personnel Department.
3 Wrong. **Are** you **working** on any special projects at the moment?
4 Right.
5 Wrong. I was working for an international head-hunting agency, when Manpower **recruited** me.
6 Right.
7 Wrong. When **did** you **join** Manpower?
8 Wrong. I **have worked/have been working** there **for** three years.
9 Wrong. I've planned a series of assessment centres I **am running/run** the first one on 1 August.
10 Right.
11 Right.
12 Wrong. If the dates of the assessment seminars **are** changed, I **will** let you know immediately./If the dates of the assessment seminars **were** changed, I would let you know immediately./If the dates of the assessment seminars **are** changed, I would let you know immediately.

Exercise 2 (M)

1 GloboPaint was established more than 100 years ago in a small workshop near Great Hammerton.
2 Today it employs more than 5,000 people in a worldwide operation with offices in more than 30 countries.
3 In fact, it is still expanding.
4 The original company, called Hammer Paints, was started by two brothers who were working as engineers.
5 They had done some market research before they set up Hammer Paints.
6 Their results showed that there was a clear need for more effective industrial paints.
7 So, initially they concentrated on just one product.
8 Today they manufacture a range of more than 250 paints as well as other oil-based products.
9 In fact, if they had not diversified, they would not have survived.
10 During the company's hundred-year history, the organisation has seen many changes in production techniques.
11 The next generation of paints will be entirely produced by computer-controlled equipment.
12 As GloboPaint knows, if they don't invest in new processes they won't be able to compete.
13 Henry Hutchison, the company's chief executive officer, said at a recent meeting, 'GloboPaint is not going to stand still.'

UNIT 10

Exercise 1 (M)

Interviewer: How do you do?
Candidate: How do you do?
Interviewer: And how was the drive?
Candidate: Fairly quick. Not too much traffic.
Interviewer: How long did it take?
Candidate: Just one and a half hours.
Interviewer: So, I'd like to ask you about your education first. What languages did you specialise in at school?
Candidate: English and French.
Interviewer: And have you used/do you use them regularly?
Candidate: Yes, quite regularly in my last job at Copert.
Interviewer: And did you use them in Spartia?
Candidate: No, not at all. All our clients were in Germany.
Interviewer: So, why did you leave Spartia?
Candidate: Because there was no possibility of an international career.
Interviewer: And why did you choose Copert?
Candidate: Because they offered me a job in the international department.
Interviewer: So, why do you want to leave Copert?
Candidate: Because I don't think there is a chance for me to progress.
Interviewer: So what are you looking for in our company?
Candidate: Basically a challenge and the opportunity to learn more about marketing.

Exercise 2

Interviewer: OK, Ms Straub, we **are conducting** interviews all week for this post. In fact, I **have interviewed** eight candidates already and I **am seeing** three more today and tomorrow. After we **have interviewed** all the candidates, we **will make** a quick decision and **will let** our first choice know by the end of next week. We **intend/are intending** to have the whole process finished in two weeks' time. Now, if we **offered** you the job, when **would** you **be able to/could** you start?
Candidate: I **will need** to give one month's notice to my current employer and then, of course, I **will need** a little time to arrange a move here. Initially I **could** commute.
Interviewer: **Do you have** any further questions at the moment?
Candidate: No, nothing else. You **have answered** all my questions.
Interviewer: Well, if you **think** of anything else, **don't hesitate** to call me.

Exercise 1

Andreas: Are we ready to begin?

Bill: Yes, let's start. <u>To think about</u> **(Thinking about/Looking at)** the agenda, my view is it won't be possible to think about every point today. We should <u>to</u> concentrate on the main item. **(delete)**

Andreas: I'm prepared <u>agreeing</u> **(to agree)**, if we all think that… it is the main item.

Cathy: The main thing, yes. Let's <u>to</u> concentrate on that. (delete)

Andreas: Right, that's agreed. By <u>to leave</u> **(leaving)** the discussion of Crystal Brothers, we can <u>to</u> finish the main business. (delete)

Bill: Okay. Then I'd like to introduce the main discussion today.

Andreas: Er, yes, can I suggest <u>to break</u> **(we break)** for coffee at 10?

Bill: Coffee! Good idea. Coffee at 10.

Cathy: Right, Andreas, it's not worth <u>to go</u> **(going)** through the report in detail. We've all read it.

Andreas: Of course. I don't want to waste time reading it to you.

Exercise 2

Travelling to America? Global Air can **take** you to over 100 American and Latin American cities, without you or your luggage **changing** airline on the way. Don't risk **missing** your connections, avoid **complicating** your trip. No other airline makes **flying** to America such a pleasure. Travel should be fun, Global Air makes it wonderful.

Exercise 3

I'd like **to see** you later today. The MD has suggested **going** to Japan next week. I'm having difficulty **persuading** him that we need more time **to prepare** our presentation. I'd appreciate **knowing** your views. Do you think we should **postpone** the trip?

UNIT 12

Exercise 1

As you may **be** aware from reports in the national media, the Board of Directors of Vida Assurance is planning **to raise** extra capital from existing shareholders through a rights issue. We recommend this option as the best way **to guarantee** the long-term security of the company. It is also our belief that the offer of additional shares will be an attractive investment, and we are sure you will agree it is worth **investing** extra money in the company.

As is normal with rights issues, the shares will be available at a low price, **offering** an excellent investment opportunity. In **recommending** them to you, we believe we have both the company's best interests and yours at heart.

Of course, the Board does not wish **to hold** a rights issue without the support of shareholders. We invite you **to express** your views on this policy at an extraordinary general meeting on 24 October at the National Exhibition Centre, or by **returning** the form enclosed with this letter.

Exercise 2

The preferred route for **shipping** our products to Europe is by air from Tokyo to London. We have successfully used this route for seven years. **To have used** alternative routes in the past would have required more complicated distribution arrangements. Until now, our European distribution operations have centred on the UK. **Changing/To change** this does not seem appropriate at the moment, but we can **look at** alternatives. It is certainly worth **finding out** the costs of **opening** a new distribution centre in southern Europe. We agreed **to set up** a committee **to investigate.**

UNIT 13

Exercise 1

<u>To have buy</u> **(To have bought)** the machine would have been a mistake. We wanted <u>that we were able to pay</u> **(to pay/to be able to pay)** over three years. AGF would not <u>permit</u> **(allow)** us <u>having</u> **(to have)** this type of arrangement.

Exercise 2

Pedro: Now, about these tests. We **tried testing** the product last week but the machinery was faulty so the results were unreliable.

Bob: I **recall having** a problem with this test last time.

Pedro: If we **stopped being** so worried about tests, we would develop new products more quickly.

Bob: On the contrary, I **like to think** that we're very concerned about quality.

Pedro: If you **stopped to think about** how much money we spend on testing, you'd be shocked.

Bob: Not at all. So long as we **go on introducing** new products, we'll carry on testing them.

Exercise 3

S: Good morning, SAWA Enterprises.

A: Hello, I'd like **to speak** to Mr Hashimoto.

S: Who's calling, please?

A: Andreas Blöm, from Salzburg. I wonder if I could **see** him this week?

S: I'm sorry, Mr Hashimoto is not free this week. He tried **to phone** you last week but you were in New York.

A: Yes, I'm sorry. I remember **asking** him to call me, but I forgot **to tell** him I would be away.

S: Perhaps I can ask him **to call** you as soon as he is free next week.

A: Yes, please do. I'll look forward **to hearing** from him.

S: Okay. Thank you for **calling**. We'll talk again next
  week.
A: Fine. Bye for now.
S: Goodbye.

UNIT 14

Exercise 1

1	c	2	a	3	a
4	b	5	b		

Exercise 2 (M)

I asked him to see Kroll.
They allow us a 10 per cent discount.
They persuaded me to accept their offer.
I tried to call you yesterday.
We suggest running a training programme.

Exercise 3

They liked having an on-site demonstration and
suggested **having the machine on trial.**
They persuaded us to cut our price. They wanted **us
to accept their payment terms.** The last point was
impossible for us. We did not expect **them to be so
uncompromising.**

UNIT 15

Exercise 1

Marina: Do you think **Kit'll** arrive during the day or
  in the evening?
Paul: He should be with you by mid-day.
Marina: Good. **We'll** have lunch together. Shall I
  book a restaurant?
Paul: **That'd** be nice.
Marina: Please ask him to ask for me at reception
  when he arrives.
Paul: **I'll** tell him that, of course.
Marina: And tell him **it'd** be good if he brought a
  copy of the Arrow report.
Paul: He **should've** sent it to you already.
Marina: Okay. Perhaps **you'd** ask him to check.
Paul: **I'll** do that.

Exercise 2

The development phase of Arpanol ends on Friday
this week. The next phase, licensing, **will begin** next
week. The final report on clinical trials **should** be
finished this month. Of course we **shall** send a copy to
all the laboratories who helped with the tests. The
drug **should** be licensed by the FDA early next year
and, once licensed, **will** be sold internationally. It **will**
be available in liquid and tablet form.

Exercise 3

1 There **should be** a 10 per cent increase on last year.
2 **Shall I give** you a written summary of the targets
  for each region?

3 The competition **will not be/won't be less** than
  last year.
4 As a new initiative, **I'd like you to send me a
  report at the end of each week.**
5 We **should have** done this last year.
6 **We should have** a good season in the urban areas.

UNIT 16

Exercise 1

1 'Paula, **will you** explain the details of the contract
  to me?'
2 '**Shall I help you**, Tom?'
3 'It **should be in the operating** manual.'
4 '**Shall I arrange a meeting with** Agos next week?'
5 '**Shall I get you** a drink of something?'
6 'They **wouldn't accept my request for
  better terms.**'
7 'You **should write to the supplier.**'
8 'All visitors **shall/should report to Security**
  on arrival.'

Exercise 2

'Will John arrive this morning?'
'No, **he won't.**'
'What about later today?'
'If the trains are running on time, he**'ll be** here
after lunch.'
'Is Mary coming too?'
'No, she said she **wouldn't come** this time.'
'What about next month?'
'Yes, she **will.**'
'**Shall** I ask Henry to see John today?'
'Yes, he **should** see him, I think.'

Exercise 3

Wilhelm: **Will** the packaging design be different from
  the old one?
Jake: Yes – and the machine**'ll** have to be modified.
Wilhelm: **Shall** I do that?
Jake: No, we **should** get Abacus to do it. They
  said they **would.**
Wilhelm: **Won't** that be expensive?
Jake: No, it **shouldn't** be.

UNIT 17

Exercise 1

1	RP	2	FP	3	PP		
4	A	5	A	6	P	7	A

Exercise 2

Journalist: May I ask, Minister, are you concerned
  about the rise in inflation to 3 per cent?
Minister: Naturally, but I think you <u>can</u> **(may)** be
  surprised by the new unemployment
  figures that come out next week.
Journalist: But, can I ask you about inflation? Might
  there be a further rise next month?.

Minister:	Economics is not a science like physics or chemistry. It is possible, there <u>can</u> **(might)** be a rise next month too.
Journalist:	<u>Might</u> **(Can/Could)** you tell me, what annual inflation figure do you now expect?
Minister:	As I have said before, I <u>mightn't</u> **(can't)** make a guess on this.
Journalist:	But you are the Finance Minister!
Minister:	Yes, but may I repeat, economics is not an exact science!

Exercise 3

The takeover of ASA Autos by Dawa **could** mean job losses at ASA's main production plants in Europe. A spokesperson for Dawa said it was too early to be certain, but **there may be some redundancies**. **The company might however** increase its small car production in Europe. Dawa **cannot** meet demand for their small cars in the Far Eastern markets, so this is an obvious area where they **may** expand their activities. Industry analysts think there **could be/might be** another major takeover in the car market soon.

UNIT 18

Exercise 1

| 1 | O | 2 | A | 3 | A | 4 | NN |
| 5 | FP | 6 | RP | 7 | D | | |

Exercise 2

A: We must ( ) check the temperature control on the mixing unit.

B: No, we **needn't** do that. It must **have** been checked already. It's the first thing to look at.

A: Then it **must** have been faulty, because the manual check shows the temperature is too high.

B: It **could/might** be faulty, I agree. We **could** check it again.

Exercise 3

Further to our telephone conversation, **we must** develop a superior organic fertiliser suitable for use by organic horticultural concerns and fruiterers. We **can/could** do this within six months. **We needn't** greatly increase our research budget. In the short term, **our Righton Research Laboratory could** send us results of tests they carried out last year. In other words, **we may already have** the data we need.

In any case, **we must** develop this product as soon as possible. **We mustn't** let our competitors have this advantage.

I am away for a few days but **I might** call you on Monday.

UNIT 19

Exercise 1

| 1 | h | 2 | e | 3 | f | 4 | d |
| 5 | a | 6 | b | 7 | g | 8 | c |

Exercise 2

Authorisation for upgrading computer capability **had to** be obtained, if the costs involved **were** more than $200. Staff **could** ask section supervisors for upgrades. Supervisors **could** ask for a written request. In this case, two people **would** together present the request. Later, they **needed/had** to present a formal report on the application of the upgrade to the purchasing department.

UNIT 20

Exercise 1

We have developed a completely interactive CD-Rom package on Honey Inc. which **will** help all employees, customers and suppliers to know our company better. In fact, we **can't** imagine anyone with links to Honey who **won't** find the Honey CD Rom interesting and fun! With a simple-to-use format and a comprehensive Contents page, anyone **can** find the information they need. You **might** for example be interested in the history of the company, or its present exports partners, or research projects. You **will** find updated reports on every aspect of the company's activities, from staffing to sport and leisure opportunities, from new products to new development plans. Anyone connected with Honey **should** find plenty of interest. You **needn't** be an expert in computing, but you **must** have access to a computer, at home or at work.

Exercise 2

2 You **should** rub Dermox Gel into the hair and scalp when dry.

3 You **should** use a towel to protect the eyes during application.

4 Dermox **must** not be used in combination with shampoos.

5 There **may** be irritation in some cases/irritation **may** occur.

6 You **should** see a doctor if irritation occurs.

7 You **must** not swallow it.

8 Dermox Gel **may/can** be used for children over two years old.

9 You **needn't** use it more than once.

UNIT 21

Exercise 1 (M)

1 David Packer was born in a small town near Manchester in 1948.

2 He attended the local primary school where he was an average student.

3 He left secondary school at the age of 16 and started his first business.
4 His first success came when he signed a deal to supply Regents with silicon chips.
5 By his 21st birthday he had made his first million.
6 He then moved into retailing and opened five shops selling hifi equipment.
7 He bought the components from the Far East and assembled the goods in a central workshop.
8 Five years later he had more than 50 shops all over the UK.
9 Then he decided to diversify into other domestic appliances.
10 When he ran into competition from larger outlets he sold them many of his shops.

Exercise 2

1 A blue-collar worker is someone who works in a manual job or in a job on the factory floor.
2 A colleague is someone who works in the same department or company or profession as you.
3 A contract is a legal agreement between two people or parties.
4 A director is someone who represents the share-holders of the company on its Board of Directors.
5 A grade is the level of a job within the structure of a company's workforce.
6 A holiday is a period of time when you do not have to go to work.
7 A homeworker is a company employee who works at home.
8 A job is a position of regular paid work in a company.
9 A moonlighter is someone who has one job during the day and another at night.
10 The personnel is the total of all the people who work for a company.
11 A superior is someone who is above you in the hierarchy of an organisation.
12 A supervisor is someone who is in charge of several other (usually blue-collar) workers.

UNIT 22

Exercise 1

1 A bank statement is sent to us by the bank every month. We are sent a bank statement every month by the bank.
2 The statement is studied very carefully.
3 They are informed of any mistakes.
4 We are contacted regularly by the bank to review our business.
5 We are likely to be caused some problems by this. Some problems are likely to be caused by this.

Exercise 2 (M)

1 Cars can't/mustn't be parked.
2 Cases must be opened/inspected.
3 Information can be obtained.
4 Passports must be shown.
5 Telephone calls can be made.
6 Money can be exchanged.

7 Computers can be connected.
8 Cigarettes mustn't be smoked.

Exercise 3 (M)

1 The manufacture of boards is shown in this transparency.
2 The rods have always been bought from local suppliers.
3 Who is the quality of the raw materials checked by?
4 The rods are being cut into boards by that machine there.
5 After that the components must be inserted into the boards.
6 Last year a faster drilling machine had to be installed.
7 The benefits of faster production should be seen next year.
8 A completely new process is going to be introduced in five years.

UNIT 23

Exercise 1

1 e	2 b	3 f
4 a	5 d	6 c

Exercise 2

2 You **should have been invoiced** at the end of the month.
3 But the regulations have changed and **they could have been leased** this year.
4 Yes, there's been a mistake and you **must have been over-charged.**
5 Not at all, the bill **needn't have been paid** in advance.
6 You should have seen in our payment conditions that it **should have been paid** by cheque.
7 So do you think the order **might/could have been cancelled?**
8 It's very simple. An order **must have been placed** by someone in your organisation.
9 To receive the discount, the goods **should have been re-ordered** within 30 days.

Exercise 3

2 He is thought to have brought an accomplice with him.
3 The accomplice is not believed to have entered the house.
4 Many items of jewellery are reported to have been stolen.
5 However, the owners are felt to have helped the burglar.
6 The owners are known to have made an exaggerated insurance claim.
7 The owners are understood to have left the country last week.
8 They are not expected to return until the defendant is behind bars.

UNIT 24

Exercise 1

1 Right.
2 Right.
3 Wrong. The situation **is always** difficult at this time of year.
4 Right.
5 Wrong. **There's** still time to change the forecast for next year.
6 Wrong. The prototype **has been** under construction for the last six months.

Exercise 2

1 Business? **It's** quite simple: **it's** other people's money.
2 **Being** good in business **is** the most fascinating kind of art. … Making money **is** art and working **is** art and good business **is** the best art.
3 Deals **are** my art form.
4 Having money **is** rather like **being** a blonde. **It is** more fun but not vital.

Exercise 3

There are few people with the same charisma as Halmet Entacre. Born into a large rural family in Southern Rotaronga, **there were** many occasions when the family **was** without food. Halmet soon decided that country life **was** not for him and often said, 'One day I **am going to be** rich and famous.' But **it was** not until the Second World War that **there was** an opportunity to move to the capital. While he **was** working in a factory producing weapons, he **was** noticed by the owner. He **was** soon promoted to the position of factory manager. When the war ended he started his first business exporting clothes to the West. With the West desperate to rebuild economies, **it was** relatively easy to find markets for his goods. His clothing empire **has been** at the forefront of the Rotarongan economy for more than 40 years now. In a recent interview, Halmet said that most of his ambitions **have been/had been** fulfilled. 'Without **being** immodest, **there's** no doubt I have come a long way from my village.'

UNIT 25

Exercise 1

1 Wrong. Can I speak **to** Ivan Tyler, please?
2 Right.
3 Right.
4 Wrong. He discussed with me last week ( ) the need for a new supplier.
5 Wrong. He **said / told me** that they were dissatisfied with their present supplier.
6 Wrong. Can you **tell** him that I'll call back later.
7 Right.

Exercise 2

Interviewer: What **do** you **say** to your competitors who **speak** of your lack of environmental concern?

Bengt: Firstly, they should **talk** to the various environmental groups I support. And, secondly, they should **discuss** our record with the relevant governmental department.

Interviewer: And what will they **be told**?

Bengt: Basically, they **will say/will be told** that I have always observed all the rules and regulations.

Interviewer: But that's not what your former Managing Director **has said**. In a recent report he **spoke** of the toxic emissions from your factories.

Bengt: Please **tell** him to provide us with some proof. There's not a shred of evidence of any improper practices. My position is clear. As I **have said** on many occasions, we have nothing to hide. And I am happy to **discuss** our environmental record with the highest authorities.

Interviewer: Is it true that you **told** a reporter from the Green Lobby that you had no time for ecologists?

Bengt: Yes, but I **said** it in the context of a lot of untrue statements made in the press about my activities.

Interviewer: So, you don't deny **saying** that.

Bengt: No, absolutely not.

Exercise 3

1 As I **said** before, …
2 When we **talked** about this matter last week, …
3 As I **told** you before, …
4 Last week they **said** that …
5 When we **discussed** this matter last week, …
6 I'd like to **speak** to you again about this matter, because …
7 We can **tell** them to …

UNIT 26

Exercise 1

1	d	2	g
3	c	4	j
5	f	6	a
7	i	8	e
9	b	10	h

Exercise 2

1 The Finance Director **declared** that the cashflow situation was very serious.
2 He **warned** that there would be problems if they didn't reduce overheads.
3 They **denied** that there had been any unnecessary expenditure.
4 He **invited** them to review his proposals.
5 He **urged** them to take appropriate action.
6 He **promised** to review the figures before the next meeting.

7 He **agreed** with the MD that they should investigate the costs of outsourcing.
8 He **persuaded** them to join the company in finding a solution.
9 He **suggested** that they reduce the workforce.
10 They **refused** to accept his suggestions.

Exercise 3

> We would like to **invite** you to take part in the investment opportunity of the year. In fact we **urge** you not to miss this unique chance to make your money work for you. We **believe** that this is a once-in-a-lifetime investment. If you **agree** to set aside a small sum every month for the next five years, we **guarantee** a staggering 105 per cent interest at the end of the period. We **estimate** that this return will far outstrip the rate of inflation during the period.
>
> If you would like to participate, please **inform** us by phone or **notify** us using the reply coupon.

UNIT 27

Exercise 1

Michael: So how **was** your trip to Rotaronga?
Jenny: In fact we **had** a very interesting time. Our subsidiary is **doing** very good business at present.
Michael: How many people **have** they **got/do** they **have** working for them now?
Jenny: They've just **had** a recruitment drive and now there **are** exactly 32 people.
Michael: And what impression did you **get** of the new management?
Jenny: I must say I was very impressed. They certainly **have/have got** commitment. I think they'll **make** a great success of it.
Michael: I'm glad to hear that you **have/have got** such optimism!
Jenny: Well, yes! I'm sure they're **doing** all the right things and will **make** it work.

Exercise 2

We **got** a letter from our solicitor this morning. He says that he **has got** the report about the claim but he **is having/has had** problems arranging a meeting to discuss the terms. Our customers are claiming that the delivery **got** to France four weeks late. By that time they **did** not **have** any chance to complete the project on time, so they **got** in touch with their lawyers to cancel the shipment. Unfortunately, our solicitor **did** not **get** their letter until the beginning of this week. That's the reason why I need to **get/have** clarification of the claim.

Exercise 3

1 We **make** a good profit from our exports.
2 We **do** business all over the world.
3 We intend to **make** an effort to reach new markets next year.

4 What did you **do** at university?
5 We will **make** the last payment next week.
6 We're not here to **make** a loss!
7 The bookkeeper will **do** the books after his holidays.
8 It used to be easier to **make** money.
9 I've got to **do** some work at the office this evening.
10 I hope to **make** an agreement with a local supplier.
11 I'm sure we can **do** well.
12 What do you **do** for a living?

UNIT 28

Exercise 1

1 **eat** – all the others are verbs of perception.
2 **sound** – all the others are linked to the sense of sight.
3 **look up** is the only one which can be a phrasal verb.
4 **sound** is the only one which can't be followed by the preposition **for**.
5 **allow** – all the others can be followed by the preposition **from** and are verbs of prohibition.
6 **go up** is the only one which isn't a phrasal verb; it's a verb + preposition.

Exercise 2

If you **look at** the transparency, you'll **see** that turnover has increased by 12 per cent over the last year. At first, this rise **sounds** very encouraging for our medium-term strategy; however, this result masks the area of overheads, which, I **feel**, have grown by a disproportionate amount. This is an area which we really must **watch/look at**. Later today we will **hear** from Paul Brown, who will discuss ways of controlling costs.

Now let's **look at** the results in some specific areas. The new wine range has been well received. The verdict on the Rotarongan Chardonnay is that it **smells** very fresh with just the right bouquet of fruit blossom, although some judges said it **tasted** a little dry. The unanimous conclusion on appearance was that it has a nice colour and **looks** good in the new-style bottle. The judges were less complimentary about the advertising jingle, which they said **sounded** rather childish. We'll **listen to/hear** it again later.

Exercise 3

Extract 1
SM: Anna, do you think you could look **after** Mr Zezuli for a few minutes? I'll be right with him.
PA: Mr Zezuli, while you're waiting perhaps you'd like to look **at** our latest fabrics.
Z: Can I look **through** the catalogues? I'd like to see your whole product range first.

Extract 2
SM: Mr Zezuli, if you'd like to look **round,** we can arrange a visit to the factory. So, first I suggest that we look **round/at** the plant. Now, if you look **out of** the window, you'll see a convoy of lorries leaving the depot.

Extract 3

SM: In this corridor, you can see paintings of the directors. This is the present MD. I've always looked **up to** her, because I think she manages the company efficiently.

Extract 4

Z: I'm afraid I'm not happy with these figures. We should look **into/through/at** them in more detail.

SM: So, I hope you'll find these more acceptable.

Z: Yes, I do. So, now let's look **ahead to** my next visit and make some provisional plans.

SM: Yes, Mr Zezuli, I look **forward to** meeting you on your next visit to Rotaronga. Let's...

UNIT 29

Exercise 1

1 **remain** – all the others are resulting verbs.
2 **stop** – all the others take the particle **to**; **stop** takes the preposition **from**.
3 **forget** – all the others take the preposition **to**; **forget** takes the particle **to**.
4 **succeed** – all the others take the preposition **on**; **succeed** takes the preposition **in**.

Exercise 2

This memo is to **inform** all members of the steering committee **about** the details of the next international meeting. I shall **provide** you **with** a list of tasks that need to be done. We will **spend** a little time **on** finalising the schedule at our next internal meeting. Unfortunately, my trip to Japan will **prevent** me **from** taking part in the meeting.

I think we should **divide** the programme for the day **into** three parts.

The first session is to **welcome** our foreign guests **to** the company and to **describe** our operations **to** them. As time is short, we will need to **limit** this part **to** the essentials – of course without **excluding** any key personnel **from** the proceedings.

In the second part of the programme, we should **compare** our working practices **with** those in other companies. We have already made it clear that we intend to **replace** some practices **with** more modern ones and this could be a fruitful area for discussion.

Finally, we will **help** the participants **with** the more complex norms which need …

Exercise 3

1 Could you put me **through to** Helmut Brinkmayer, please?
2 Good morning, Mr Brinkmayer. As we are ready to proceed, I'd like to bring **forward** the date of our next meeting.
3 We're facing some problems here. Would it be possible to put delivery **back/off** till next month?
4 We're looking for someone to put some money **into** the business.
5 If we can't find some extra capital, we'll have to put the business **up** for sale.

6 I find it difficult to put **up with** this uncertainty.
7 We need to make a decision today. We can't put it **off** any longer.

UNIT 30

Exercise 1

1 Right.
2 Wrong. Don't worry if you can't find the letter now. You can look **for** it later.
3 Wrong. Did you **watch/see** that programme on the TV last night?
4 Right.
5 Wrong. I'll pick **you up** at your hotel at 7 o'clock, if that suits you.
6 Wrong. We can discuss ( ) the proposals over dinner.
7 Wrong. I'll ask ( ) my secretary to fax you the documents this afternoon.
8 Right.

Exercise 2

Bill: Nigel! How are you **getting on**?
Nigel: Fine, thanks, Bill.
Bill: I hear you recently **gave up** working for Alpha.
Nigel: Yes, they **turned down** my application for the post of Marketing Manager.
Bill: So did they **take on** someone from outside?
Nigel: Yes, though in the end I was glad to **get away from** Alpha. It **turned out** to be a good move.
Bill: Really!
Nigel: While I was deciding what to do, I **came across** an old friend from university. And he **put forward** a number of very interesting work ideas. And in the end I **filled in** an ad in the paper for a franchise, called CLSS.
Bill: And what does that abbreviation **stand for**?
Nigel: Criminal Lawyer Support Services.

Exercise 3

1 We tried to find a replacement for Fred, but finally we decided to take him **back.**
2 Why don't you take **down** that old sign? It looks terrible.
3 It's recruitment time. We are taking **on** a number of new junior managers at the moment.
4 That product is a real success; it has taken **off** in a big way.
5 We are conducting a survey. It won't take **up** more than a few minutes of your time.
6 We expect that BusCom will try to take us **over** in the near future.

UNIT 31

Exercise 1

	Simple sentence	Complex sentence connected by		
		coordination	subordination	general purpose connector
Statement	9	8	3,4	6
Question	1,5		2	
Command	7,12	10		
Exclamation	11			

Exercise 2 (M)

UNIT 32

Exercise 1

H	I	O	P	L	K	B	V	T	Y	U	I	F
G	G	Y	J	U	Y	N	L	Y	P	A	O	I
L	U	Q	Q	P	U	A	K	J	O	S	I	N
O	W	P	P	T	O	C	T	S	L	H	Y	A
P	R	N	O	H	P	T	U	I	I	O	H	L
L	I	A	E	E	M	U	B	M	U	W	N	L
A	L	T	E	R	N	A	T	I	V	E	L	Y
S	G	U	Y	E	W	L	A	L	L	V	M	P
T	J	R	R	F	A	L	E	A	K	E	B	O
L	L	A	B	O	S	Y	R	R	H	R	V	L
Y	O	L	N	R	D	E	Y	L	T	D	C	K
E	P	L	M	E	F	A	N	Y	W	A	Y	J
U	Q	Y	A	W	G	L	I	A	R	F	X	M
P	T	U	R	I	N	S	T	E	A	D	A	N
Q	J	I	T	P	H	O	C	E	E	H	S	V

Exercise 2 (M)

If you need a challenge, **then** our **ADVENTURE HOLIDAYS** could be the answer.

Our weekend programmes provide opportunities for developing leadership qualities within a tough **but/yet** supportive group environment. **In other words,** we'll sharpen you up as an individual **as well as** making you into a top-class team player.

The weekend is spent at our training centre in the beautiful Lake District. **Naturally/obviously,** you'll want some comfort, **so** we've taken over a small castle, but **to start with** you'll have to get past the guards.

We start on a Friday evening without dinner. **Then/after that** there is an orientation session. **After that/Then** it's down to business. You'll spend most of your weekend outside, working with others on a variety of intellectually and physically challenging activities. **However/But** there's a warm bed waiting for you after you've finished the course.

You can expect to return home on Sunday evening a changed person, **in other words/that is to say** ready to face any new challenges.

Also, we hope you'll **then** return for another **ADVENTURE WEEKEND** at some future date. **However,** most of our graduates find that they don't need to.

UNIT 33

Exercise 1

1. I always read the Financial Times while **(I)** am having my breakfast.
2. I especially study it **to** find the details of the share prices.
3. I like to find out how **my shares are doing.**
4. Recently I decided to sell some shares because **( )** they were performing badly.
5. **If** I had known that they would recover, I wouldn't have sold them.
6. I used the money to invest in a Rotarongan company **which** promised a good return.
7. Although **( )** the company literature said it was a safe investment, it went bankrupt.
8. After **losing** my money there, I chose a more established company.
9. **As** they say, a fool and his money are soon parted.
10. To **summarise,** it was a bitter experience which taught me an unforgettable lesson.

Exercise 2

1. <u>While customs are different around the world,</u> good manners are appreciated everywhere.
2. Kordab Bronsaw is a Rotarongan sociologist <u>who has studied various societies.</u>
3. On the subject of Rotaronga, he has said <u>that local habits are very easy to follow.</u>
4. Rotarongans have had a lot of contact with foreigners, <u>so they understand different cultures.</u>
5. Kordab has written a short guide <u>so that visitors to the country will know how to behave.</u>
6. <u>If you are invited for dinner,</u> come on time.
7. Guests should bring a small gift <u>when they are invited to a person's house.</u>
8. <u>Because Rotarongans are very hospitable,</u> your glass and plate will always be full.
9. Your hosts will be inquisitive and will want to know <u>what you think of their country.</u>

Reported question	Condition	Time	Relative clause	Contrast	Purpose	Reported speech	Cause	Result
9	6	7	2	1	5	3	8	4

Exercise 3

1 b	**2** e	**3** a	
4 d	**5** f	**6** c	

UNIT 34

Exercise 1

1 **because** does not indicate contrast.
2 **what** is not a relative pronoun.
3 **for to** is not grammatically correct.
4 **if** does not indicate time.
5 **whereas** does not indicate condition.

Exercise 2 (M)

1 ABC is a small engineering company making pumps.
2 When the recession hit the building industry, we saw our orders declining.
3 Although we cut back on the workforce, this was not enough to protect our position.
4 After we saw/seeing the benefits of introducing a quality system, we started a project to investigate the advantages ourselves.
5 Because we needed to improve quality we asked the production line workers to contribute suggestions.
6 We set up a number of quality circles in order to find out how the quality of our manufacturing processes could be improved.
7 Some of the workers' ideas were accepted whereas others were rejected.
8 As soon as quality improved, we saw an increase in our customers.
9 Having consolidated our position, we are now ready to expand again.

Exercise 3

As/Because/Since living and working in London has become more expensive and less pleasant and **as/because/since** we need to expand, we have decided to move our operations to York next year. **While/(Al)though** York will not offer the range of facilities of the capital, we are sure that it will provide the right working environment **so that/in order that** the company can thrive. **In order to/So as to/To** maintain contact with our customers, we have been building up a database and would be grateful **if** you could check that your details are correct. Please be sure to return the form to us in the envelope provided **so that/in order that** we can update our records and keep you informed. **When** we move, we intend to pass on the savings to our valued clients and **as soon as when** we are installed we shall be writing to you again telling you of our exciting new developments.

UNIT 35

Exercise 1

S	A	F	H	I	L	U	B	N	D	W	E
R	T	D	E	S	C	R	I	B	E	E	T
G	U	I	O	P	K	G	E	T	C	R	I
A	S	A	G	R	E	E	T	Y	L	K	D
C	B	N	I	O	P	L	K	J	I	E	E
C	O	N	F	I	R	M	A	S	N	D	C
Q	U	O	T	H	J	I	K	T	E	L	L
C	S	U	G	G	E	S	T	L	O	P	A
C	U	N	A	S	D	F	O	I	W	P	R
B	A	C	P	G	O	L	S	T	A	T	E
E	R	E	F	U	S	E	H	I	R	E	T
A	C	D	E	E	F	K	I	L	N	T	I
G	O	I	L	S	N	I	M	R	T	E	Y
A	D	V	I	S	E	A	F	R	A	H	Y

Exercise 2 (M)

1 The Marketing Director suggested introducing the new measures immediately.
2 The Finance Director asked if they had calculated the final figures.
3 The Personnel Manager warned them to be careful with recruitment.
4 The Managing Director promised that he'd review/to review the situation the following week.
5 The Production Manager announced that he was going to resign.
6 The R & D Manager threatened to sell the patents if he didn't get his extra budget.
7 The Chairman of the Board recommended that the company (should) appoint a new management team.

UNIT 36

Exercise 1

1 Wrong. In the meeting we advised **him/her/them** to invest more money in research.
2 Right.
3 Wrong. They asked how much money **we needed.**
4 Right.
5 Wrong. They agreed **to look** at the figures again.
6 Right.
7 Wrong. He asked us **not to reveal** the figures to anyone else.
8 Right.

Exercise 2

John pointed out that the company faced a serious problem and needed to cut their running costs by at least 12 per cent. He warned that if they didn't, then they might face closure.

Mary suggested looking for areas where savings could be made.

Alan stated that he couldn't agree with the proposed budget cut. He warned that if his department's budget was reduced, it would be very difficult for him to meet the targets.

John reminded him that if they couldn't make the savings, then there would be no targets to meet.

Alan replied that if his budget was cut, then there would be no products to sell. He added that unless they had the new products for the beginning of the following year, they would lose many of their customers and that then they would be in the same position as they were when they started 10 years earlier.

John answered that he revised that they faced a serious problem, but emphasised that they needed to find a workable solution.

Exercise 3

1 I asked when the new prototype would be introduced.
2 He replied that they were still testing it, but hoped to have it ready by the summer.
3 I warned that any delay could mean that our competitors might overtake us.
4 He reassured me that there was little chance of that.
5 I proposed that we fix a date for the presentation of the prototype.
6 He agreed to discuss this with the rest of the team and let me know the following week.

UNIT 37

Exercise 1

1	who?	2	what/which?
3	when?	4	where?
5	why?	6	how?
7	how long?	8	how far?
9	how much/many?	10	how big/small/long? etc.

Exercise 2

1 Wrong. Where **were** you born?
2 Right.
3 Wrong. When did you **join** your present company?
4 Wrong. How long ( ) have you worked in that department?
5 Wrong. Why **did** you **change** your job?
6 Wrong. What **happened** to the payment?
7 Wrong. I'd like to know if the payment **arrived** yesterday.
8 Wrong. I'm afraid I don't know what payment you are talking **about.**
9 Wrong. Why **didn't you** inform us earlier about this error?
10 Wrong. If ( ) you have any questions, I'll be happy to answer them.

Exercise 3

J: Paul Johnson, you've lived here for many years. But you're not from this country, are you?

Where were you born?
P: In fact I was born in a small village in Rotaronga.
J: **And when did you leave?**
P: I left when I was 15 years old.
J: **Why did you decide to leave?**
P: I decided to leave because there were very few opportunities.
J: **Where did you go?**
P: First I went to the capital.
J: **How long did you stay there?**
P: About five years.
J: And then you came here. **So how long have you lived in this country?**
P: I've lived here since the early '80s.
J: **Was it difficult to make a start here?**
P: Yes, it was very difficult to make a start here.
J: In fact you have built up a very successful retailing business. **What (projects) are you working on at the moment?**
P: At the moment we are working on a diversification plan. But at present it's secret.
J: You are one of the biggest employers in your sector. **How many people do you employ?**
P: We employ about 30,000 people.
J: You are a prolific traveller. **How many miles do you travel each year?**
P: About 250,000 miles each year, I think.
J: **How long do you plan to continue your intensive lifestyle?**
P: I plan to continue this intensive lifestyle for another few years.
J: **And what ambitions do you have?**
P: My main ambition is to return to my country and retire there.

UNIT 38

Exercise 1

1 Did you make any useful contacts during your trip?
2 Which consultants did you see during your visit to New York?
3 Who spoke to you from our foreign subsidiary?
4 When are we going to receive their order in writing?
5 Where do you think we will manage to get the extra orders from?
6 I'd like to know how long they expect us to wait.
7 How much will the total package cost us?
8 How many people will you need to install the equipment?
9 How far have we got on the current project?
10 Why didn't you inform us earlier about the problems you were facing?

Exercise 2

1 A: Could I speak to John Fowler, please.
2 B: Who's speaking, please?
3 A: My name is Elena Bronowski.
4 B: And what's it in connection with?
5 A: Sorry, what did you say?
6 B: I asked why you wanted to speak to John Fowler.
7 A: I'd like to find out if he can arrange some advertising for us.
8 B: And your name again was…?

9 A: Elena Bronowski.
10 B: I'm sorry. Could you spell that for me, please?
11 A: Yes, certainly. It's B –
12 B: For Berlin?
13 A: Yes, R-O-N-O-W-S-K-I.
14 B: Just hold on, please, Mrs Bronowski…
15 B: I'm sorry, he's in a meeting. D'you think you could call back later?
16 A: OK, but could you give me Mr Fowler's direct number?
17 B: Yes, it's 437-0028.

Exercise 3

1 Please tell us how long you have known Vassili Theodopoulos.
2 We would like to know where you last saw him.
3 We would like to ask you if you suspected anything about his company's operations.
4 The police would like to know why you didn't contact us sooner about your suspicions.
5 Could you tell us who contacted you after your last meeting with him?
6 Do you think you could tell us when you are going to Greece next?
7 I wonder if you'd mind telling us if you will be visiting his offices in Athens.
8 I was wondering if we could ask you if you have ever been involved in any illegal activities.

UNIT 39

Exercise 1

A	C	C	O	M	M	O	D	A	T	I	O	N	S
D	W	A	E	R	T	Y	I	O	L	P	T	K	D
V	B	S	U	G	G	E	S	T	I	O	N	M	E
I	A	E	G	H	L	Q	N	M	Y	T	R	E	V
C	S	T	R	E	L	U	G	G	A	G	E	L	I
E	C	R	I	T	E	I	F	L	I	G	R	E	C
S	T	R	T	R	I	P	P	E	T	A	B	L	E
A	R	O	U	M	E	M	E	E	R	P	A	O	L
F	A	S	H	O	T	E	L	T	A	Y	O	R	L
C	F	T	O	P	M	N	T	R	V	A	R	R	S
D	F	U	R	N	I	T	U	R	E	A	T	Y	R
B	I	G	H	D	E	T	H	Y	L	I	A	N	B
S	C	V	U	I	L	M	N	Q	U	E	R	T	G

hotel, accommodation
device, equipment
suggestion, advice
lorry, traffic
trip, travel
case, luggage
table, furniture

Exercise 2

In this bulletin I would like to give you the most recent **information** about the company's finances. Since the acquisition by Megacorp our **assets have** risen by 65 per cent and our **debts have** fallen by 25 per cent. Megacorp have provided us with additional **funds** which we can use to develop the business and have given us **permission** to use this money as we see fit. The financial restructuring has involved a lot of **work** and **travel** and I should like to extend **thanks** to the whole management team who have been so supportive during this difficult period. The future of the company is now secured and we will be looking to moving our **headquarters** to York in the near future. This will enable us to release some of our **capital** and reduce our **liabilities.**

Exercise 3

1	c	2	f	3	i	4	j
5	a	6	d	7	b	8	e
9	g	10	h				

UNIT 40

Exercise 1

1 asset management
2 an insurance claim
3 a company balance sheet
4 a salesman
5 an overseas subsidiary
6 a government subsidy
7 a shareholder
8 a majority shareholder
9 a company car
10 a production technique study
11 a management progress report
12 a computer component manufacturer

Exercise 2

1 market research department
2 employee relations department
3 new product research department
4 employee welfare department
5 data processing services department
6 contract drafting department
7 quality control department
8 customer relations department

Exercise 3

The **paper producers** are celebrating **record prices and profits. Forestry industry groups** have surprised **city analysts** with bumper earnings. One **newsprint producer** has moved from loss to profit in one year. Of course, **price increases** have helped and further **price rises** are in the pipeline. The **paper market buoyancy** is reflected in **price hikes** for **laser printer and photocopier paper. Cost-cutting measures** in the industry have also led to better figures. But producers are worried about **paper conservation measures** which could have an impact on consumption.

UNIT 41

Exercise 1

Microcorp

Balance sheet	as at 31 December 19 ___	(statement of company's position at a certain date)

ASSETS	£000	(things belonging to the company)
Fixed assets		(property/equipment owned by the company)
Land	340	(ground)
Buildings	120	(factory, offices, etc.)
Plant & machinery	100	(equipment)
Total fixed assets	560	
Current assets		(items used by the company in their ordinary work)
Raw material		(substances for use in manufacturing)
Work in progress	140	(value of goods being manufactured)
Finished goods		(manufactured goods ready for sale)
Debtors	35	(persons owing money to the company)
Cash in hand at bank	35	(money deposited at bank)
Total current assets	210	
Current liabilities		(debts which the company must pay in the next accounting period)
Creditors	50	(people owed money)
Bank overdraft	30	(money owed to the bank)
Taxation	30	(taxes)
Total current liabilities	110	
Net current assets	100	
(working capital)		
Net assets	660	

UNIT 42

Exercise 1

1 a decision-maker
2 the decision of the board *or* the board's decision
3 an information-gathering meeting
4 useful advice
5 yesterday's fax
6 five pieces of equipment
7 a price quotation
8 the sales manager
9 the company's results *or* the secretary's minutes
10 the company's results

Exercise 2

Yesterday's proceedings, starting with the company's extraordinary meeting, were held in the visitors' meeting room. The morning's agenda started with the Chairman's introductory speech, confirming that the first two quarters' results had been better than expected. 'It's with great pleasure that I present these figures; I hadn't expected them to be quite so good.' The shareholders' views were well represented by some 250 participants. The shareholders' main concerns were with the company's plans to diversify into new areas such as software development. George Armstrong felt that the company's strength was its very weakness. 'I wouldn't move into new areas now; there's a lot of consolidation to be done first.' However, the Chairman, emphasising the need to take the initiative, pointed to other firms' successes in these areas, particularly last month's launch of Microm's Opsys 95, claimed to be every organisation's solution to system crashes. The members' views were, however, mixed.

UNIT 43

Exercise 1

1 interestingly
2 economically
3 rapidly
4 gradually
5 dramatically
6 well
7 healthily
8 excellently

Exercise 2

The economical **(economic)** case for increasing investment in tourism is good, but the most recently **(recent)** figures available show a slower growth in tourism in most areas. For this reason, we should introduce changes gradual **(gradually)** and only with careful consideration of future trends. An important factor will be exchange rates. With a strong currency, we can expect fewer foreign visitors. As tourism becomes increasing **(increasingly)** important, the government should think about the effects of a strongly **(strong)** currency on tourism and employment in the touristic **(tourist)** industry.

Exercise 3

1 The use of recycled paper is **ecologically** desirable.
2 **Economic** considerations are also important.
3 Recycled paper is often **cheap.**
4 Most companies report a **high** level of interest in environmental issues.
5 Consumers prefer to think they are **kind** to animals.
6 Consumers **hardly** notice the small print on a bottle of shampoo.

Exercise 4

The **first** thing you can notice here is the **considerable** fall in grain production over the past four years. This is almost **wholly** due to a return to **traditional** farming methods. You can see, for example, that the **broken** line shows a drop in the use of **chemical** fertilisers. This change in farming methods, **mainly** as a consequence of **environmental** pressure, has affected agricultural production in several areas. It has **naturally** had important **economic** effects on the farmers.

UNIT 44

Exercise 1

Helga:	Was it a **reasonably** successful fair?
Ulrike:	Well, yes, it was **quite** a worthwhile couple of days. We made some **fairly** unexpected contacts.
Helga:	So, good news! Some new business?
Ulrike:	Yes, in fact, some areas where we're **virtually** unknown.
Helga:	Good, because without new contacts these fairs can be an **extremely** expensive exercise.

Exercise 2

1 Wrong. The latest semi-conductors are **extremely** small.
2 Wrong. The amount of information that can be included on a chip is **(quite/absolutely)** enormous.
3 Wrong. The cost of hardware is **considerably** lower than it used to be.
4 Wrong. Every year brings **( )** significant improvements in system capability.
5 Right.

Exercise 3

'The continued rise in our share price has been **very** beneficial to the board, enabling us to raise money for further capital investment. This has been **extremely** useful, giving us a better basis for future growth. The stock market has noticed our **highly** prudent investment policies. And consequently, investors have felt **quite** confident about our ability to give a good return on their investments. All of this proves that we are **reasonably** justified in expecting further success in the future.'

UNIT 45

Exercise 1 (M)

1 Arrow has had a slightly larger turnover this year than last year.
2 Arrow has produced moderately better results this year.
3 Harry's shows a considerably increased share price.
4 Last year Harry's turnover was fractionally less than Arrow.
5 Now, Harry's turnover is considerably higher.
6 Harry's share price has reached a highly respectable 78 pence.
7 There is now a substantial difference between the two companies.
8 Last year there was little significant difference.
9 Harry's now has a much greater turnover than Arrow.
10 Arrow, however, has had a moderately successful year.

Exercise 2

J: How do you compare gas as a source of power with alternative methods of energy generation?
PK: Well, gas is **a much more economical source of power** than alternative forms.
J: Isn't wind **a better** alternative?
PK: No, wind isn't **better.** It is much **more expensive** and **more destructive** of the environment. Wind farms are ugly, no-one wants them.
J: So do you think more gas-fired power can actually improve the environment?
PK: Yes, gas is certainly **cleaner than** coal and **safer than** nuclear power.
J: Well, thank you, Mr Kelving.

UNIT 46

Exercise 1

| 1 F | 2 F | 3 T | 4 F |
| 5 T | 6 T | 7 T | |

Exercise 2

| 1 e | 2 d | 3 b |
| 4 c | 5 a | |

Exercise 3

I: What sort of promotion usually works best for your type of goods, for DIY products?
MD: Well, first of all, we **rarely** use on-pack promotions. We find that there are **more effective** ways to promote our products. We **usually** have in-store demonstrations, so customers can see exactly how the product works. This makes a **greater** impression.
I: What about competitions, or free offers?
MD: No, we **never** use methods like that. That might be okay for **cheaper** goods, but ours are high-quality products. The customer knows that if he or she wants the best, then they pay for it, but there are **seldom** any extras. It's the best product to do the job. Simply that!

UNIT 47

Exercise 1

So far as we are aware, we have not been paid for the above invoice. If you are unhappy about our invoice for some reason, please call us to discuss the problem. Unfortunately, we have now waited long **enough**. It is **such** a long time since we sent the invoice and the payment is **so** late, that we are forced to consider legal action. I am sure you would not wish to incur **very** high legal fees on top of the amount already owed.

Since we are always prepared to help our customers, you may be interested to know that it is not **too** late to negotiate different payment terms. Please contact us to discuss this option.

Exercise 2

1 The distance between the handlebar and the brake is **not wide enough**.
2 The saddle is **too narrow**; it should be 15 cms.
3 The rubber on the handlebars is **not soft enough**.
4 **It is surprising** that **such** a light frame is **so** strong.
5 **Such** high-quality materials may demand a price **that is too high**.
6 **So long as** the improvements are made quickly, the bike will be ready for Christmas.

UNIT 48

Exercise 1

1 Model A has always been **the best** seller. After one year, A had **already** reached 300 and sales rose in the second year and **again** last year. However, A has probably **already** peaked, but we do expect that next year it will sell **as** much **as** this year.
2 Sales of model B started well and were **already** at 300 by last year. Although sales are **still** at 300 units this year, they are expected to rise **again** next year.
3 Model C has always been **the weakest** performer. Sales have **already** fallen and will fall **again** next year. We have not **yet** made a decision on future marketing of C, but it has always sold **less than** we expected, so we may drop it.

Exercise 2

Thank you for your letter concerning the information given on our food packaging.

You will be glad to know that in line with government regulations we **already** give detailed lists of ingredients on all the packaging of our products. We do not **yet** provide details of how the foods are produced but we do have plans to give this information as well. We are **still** involved in research to find the best way to give this information. **As soon as** we reach a decision, we will begin labelling all our foods with details of where and how the foods are produced.

Once **again**, thank you for your concern.

UNIT 49

Exercise 1 (suggested answers)

If I am at home, I get up at 6.30.

I wash; then I go for **a** jog before breakfast.

After **the** jog, I have **a** shower.

Then I eat breakfast – usually **a** bowl of cereal.

During breakfast, I read **a/the** newspaper.

Then I get **the** car from **the** garage and drive to **the** office.

The journey takes about 20 minutes.

When I arrive at **the** office, first I look at **the** post and **the** e-mail.

I have **a** very good secretary who plans and organises **the** timetable for me.

I travel to Spain about three times **a** month.

I like working with **the** Spanish because they enjoy life – both **the** professional and **the** social side.

In Madrid I often go to **the** theatre or **a** concert.

At home, in **the** evening I usually watch **the** news on **(the)** TV before going to bed.

Exercise 2

Sumita CD-ROM drives are designed to provide countless hours of trouble-free operation without maintenance. However, problems do sometimes occur, though most of them are easy to solve without **a** great deal of technical expertise. So, if **a** problem does occur, **the** first step is to make sure that **the** software has been properly installed; you will see **an** error message on **(the)** screen when you start up **the** machine if something has not been correctly installed. If **the** problem persists, check **the** following items:

If the disc tray does not open:

- is **the** power cord connected?
  is **the** power switch turned to **the** ON position? You will see **a** short flash of light from **the** front panel when **the** drive is powered up. Remember that **the** disc tray will not move without supplying power.

- If **the** disc tray does not move even when **the** power is supplied, turn **the** power switch to **the** OFF position and turn **the** emergency knob in **an** anti-clockwise direction while pressing with **a** small screwdriver. Then **the** disc tray will open **a** little way. Carefully pull **the** disc tray open and close **the** disc tray again.

- After closing **the** disc tray, turn **the** power switch to ON and check **the** tray operates correctly.

If **the** tray now operates correctly, insert **a** disk and read section 4 in **the** booklet.

And remember, discs should always be stored in their cases when not in use to keep them free from dirt and dust.

UNIT 50

Exercise 1

1 International business may conduct its operations with scraps of paper, but **the** ink it uses is human blood.
2 Executives are like joggers. If you stop **a** jogger, he goes on running on **the** spot. If you drag **an** executive away from his business, he goes on running on **the** spot, pawing **the** ground, talking business.
3 Corporation. **An** ingenious device for obtaining individual profit without individual responsibility.
4 It is **the** interest of **the** commercial world that wealth should be found everywhere.
5 **A** client is to me **a** mere unit, **a** factor in **a** problem.
6 It is very vulgar to talk about one's business. Only people like stockbrokers do that, and then merely at dinner parties.
7 What's good for **the** country is good for General Motors, and vice versa.

Exercise 2

2 **d** A crime is **a** wrong done to **the** State which is dealt with by means of **(a)** prosecution.

3 **f** Damages are **the** financial compensation awarded to **an** innocent party for **a** breach of duty/**the** breach of **a** duty.

4 **i** A duty is **an** obligation owed by one person to another.

5 **c** Goods are **the** subject matter of **a** contract for **the** sale of goods.

6 **b** A judgement is **the/an** actual decision of **the/a** court in **a** particular case which settles **the** outcome of **the** case and binds **the** parties to **the** dispute.

7 **a** A merger is **the** joining together of two companies under **the** name of one of them or as **a** new company.

8 **e** A premium is **the** price paid by **the/an** insured person in **an** insurance contract.

9 **j** Remuneration is **the** payment of **a** sum of money in exchange for services.

10 **g** Title is **the** legal ownership of **(a)** property by one person.

UNIT 51

Exercise 1

1 **your** – all the others are 1st person singular.

2 **it's** is not a pronoun; it stands for **it is.**

3 **theirselves** is not correct English.

4 **me** is an object pronoun; all the others can be subject pronouns.

5 **there** is an adverb.

Exercise 2

Andrew: **I'm** not totally convinced about **our** new packaging. What do **you** think about **it**, Sylvia?

Sylvia: **I'm** reasonably happy with **it, myself. I** think the caption captures what **we** are trying to say with **our** new product. A family product – no frills. **I** think **it**'ll appeal to **our** target shopper and **she**'ll put **it** straight into **her** supermarket trolley. OK, the bottle **itself** is nothing special, but in any case **we** are aiming at the average consumer.

Andrew: Yes, but **our** average consumer has become a lot more demanding. **They** are looking for products with a distinctive style and **ours** just doesn't stand out from the crowd.

Boris: So what do **you** suggest?

Andrew: **I** think **we** are going to have to rethink the packaging. If **you** look at WashWell and Fresh Hair, **they** are both clearly identifiable by **their** packaging. **We** have always prided **ourselves** on staying ahead of the competition. So, **we** can't let **them** overtake **us** now. So, **I** recommend that **we** talk to the design team again and ask **them** to come up with a new bottle and new packaging. This is a really important product for **us** and **we**

can't afford to make any mistakes. If **you** like, **I**'ll talk to **them myself. I**'ll contact Pete Menzies first; **he** usually has some innovative ideas.

Boris: Yes, **I** think that's a good idea to ask **him.** So, please keep **me** informed of developments.

Exercise 3

1 HomeCare is a leading name in products for the home.

2 We are pleased to send you our latest catalogue of home improvements.

3 It contains a wealth of new ideas to improve the look of your house.

4 These include easy-to-install tips for the novice.

5 There are also many new products for those of you who are already experts.

6 In short, you'll find something for everyone.

7 Our products are not available on the high street.

8 You can only buy them through this catalogue.

9 As for delivery, they'll be with you next day.

10 That's our promise.

11 So, phone us today and improve your major asset.

UNIT 52

Exercise 1

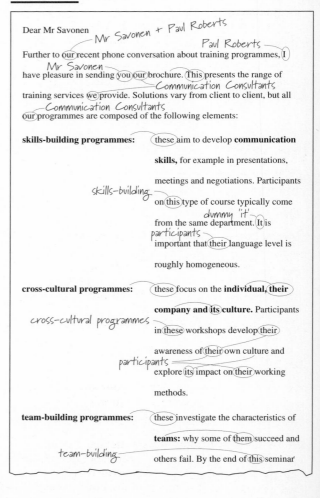

Dear Mr Savonen

Mr Savonen + Paul Roberts

Further to **our** recent phone conversation about training programmes, **I** have pleasure in sending **you our** brochure. This presents the range of training services **we** provide. Solutions vary from client to client, but all **our** programmes are composed of the following elements:

Paul Roberts
Mr Savonen
Communication Consultants
Communication Consultants

skills-building programmes: these aim to develop **communication skills,** for example in presentations, meetings and negotiations. Participants on this type of course typically come from the same department. It is important that their language level is roughly homogeneous.

skills-building
dummy "it"
participants

cross-cultural programmes: these focus on the **individual, their company and its culture.** Participants in these workshops develop their awareness of their own culture and explore its impact on their working methods.

cross-cultural programmes
participants

team-building programmes: these investigate the characteristics of **teams:** why some of them succeed and others fail. By the end of this seminar

team-building

110

individuals will have a better understanding

Paul Roberts → *individuals*

individuals → of (their) strengths and weaknesses.

given in this letter →

I hope (this) information is of interest to (you) and I look forward to speaking

Mr Savonen →

to (you) again once the needs of (your) managers have been more clearly

defined. Finally, please feel free to contact (me) if (you) would like to discuss

Paul Roberts → ← *Mr Savonen*

any of (these) programmes in more detail.

given in this letter →

Yours sincerely

Paul Roberts

Paul Roberts
Partner

Exercise 2

A: Primebuild are recruiting engineers for a construction project in SE Asia.

B: Who are **they?**

A: **They** design and construct power plants.

B: But do **they** install **them?**

A: No, **they** do all the initial construction work for water and electricity. After **that** is completed, the power generators install the equipment **itself.**

B: And **these/those** engineers… where are **they** to work exactly?

A: **This** advertisement just says SE Asia.

B: Yes, but **that** is a very large area.

A: Yes, I know **that.** But, to be honest, I'd be happy to get a job somewhere away from **this** area. **It** has too many unhappy memories for me. I've applied for too many jobs….

B: … and got none of **them.** I know **your** feeling. In fact maybe I will apply **myself.**

UNIT 53

Exercise 1

1 Let me give you **some** advice.

2 I can't find **any** information about the company.

3 I'll look **somewhere** else. It could be in another file.

4 Have you **ever** been to the Trade Fair in Dortmund?

5 I was **somewhat** confused by his presentation. It just didn't make **any** sense.

6 We'll **never** use that supplier again. They let us down terribly.

Exercise 2

Jane: Thank you very much for your attention. And now, are there **any/some** questions?

Peter: Jane, do you think that prices will **ever** return to their pre–1980 level?

Jane: Thanks for your question. In fact, I am not **at all** surprised by your concern about prices. But I am sure that prices will **never** return to those levels. The current situation of over-supply means that customers can buy stocks almost

anywhere from their traditional suppliers. In fact, having spoken to **some** of them recently, they have told me they have reached the stage where there is **nowhere** to store the surplus coal they have mined. And they simply can't do **anything** to influence the situation. In the history of the industry, we've seen **nothing** like this before. Of course, **anything/something** could happen in the future, but I think we have to be pragmatic. So, to answer your question, **no** return to earlier prices! I know that that is not **something** you like to hear, but I think it sums up the present situation. Does that answer your question?

Peter: Yes, thanks.

Jane: **Some/Any** more questions?

(No hands go up)

I'm sure there are **some** more questions! No? Well, if there are **no** more questions at the moment, I'd like to thank you for your attention, and please feel free to contact me if you'd like to discuss **any/some** of the points I raised. In **any** case, I'll be seeing **some** of you **some time** later today in our small working groups.

Exercise 3

A: Could you put me through to **someone** in your accounts department, please.

B: Is there **anyone/someone** in particular you'd like to speak to?

A: No, but it's in connection with **some** bills we have received.

B: Just one moment, and I'll connect you to Mr Kempton. (Pause)

I'm afraid there's **no-one** there at the moment. But, if you hold, I'll just check if I can find him **somewhere/anywhere** in the building.

A: Actually, I've got **some** other phone calls to make now. So, I'd appreciate if you could ask **someone** to phone me.

B: **Any** particular time?

A: **Some/Any** time this afternoon, please.

B: Fine, I'll do that.

A: Can you give me your name, please?

B: Yes, it's…

UNIT 54

Exercise 1

1 Wrong. We are not interested in **any** new equipment at the moment.

2 Right.

3 Wrong. I haven't told **anybody** yet about the new contract.

4 Right.

5 Right.

6 Wrong. Don't do **anything** until you have spoken to a lawyer.

Exercise 2

HL: Is there any message on screen when you start the system?
KA: Yes, it says 'virus detected'.
HL: And does it say anything after that?
KA: Yes, then it says 'Do you want to continue?'
HL: And has any new software been installed on the system?
KA: No, absolutely nothing.
HL: And does anyone apart from the authorised users use the system?
KA: No, no-one at all.
KA: So, is there anything that you can do to solve the problem over the phone?
HL: No, I don't think so.
KA: So, when can you send someone over?
HL: If you hang on, I'll just check if we have anyone anywhere in your area.
KA: We really need someone to come over today.
HL: OK, I'll make sure we send someone over some time this afternoon.

Exercise 3

CO: Good morning, sir. Could I see your passport, please.
AD: Yes, here you are.
CO: Have you **ever** visited Rotaronga before?
AD: No, I've **never** been here before.
CO: And is this all your luggage? Do you have **anything** else?
AD: No, this is everything.
CO: And are you carrying **anything** for **anyone/someone** else?
AD: No, this is all mine.
CO: Do you have **anything** to declare? **Any** wine, spirits, cigarettes?
AD: No, **nothing**.
CO: Fine. And have you booked **somewhere/ anywhere** to stay here in Rotaronga?
AD: No, not yet. I was hoping to book **somewhere** downtown from the airport.
CO: Actually, as far as I know, **none** of the big hotels have any spare rooms, but it just so happens that my brother runs a nice, clean pension very close to the centre. Are you **at all** interested? Anyway, here's his card.

UNIT 55

Exercise 1

1 We produce all ( ) kinds of textiles.
2 ( ) Most of them are made from natural products.
3 Many of **the** raw materials come from New Zealand.
4 How **much** do you pay per tonne?
5 The price depends on **lots/a lot** of different factors.
6 In the past we used to pay just a **little** money for synthetics, but this has increased a lot recently.
7 Of course, we have several ( ) competitors.
8 Only a **few** of them are in this country, because labour costs here are so high.

9 We don't expect **any** further price increases in raw materials this year.

Exercise 2

HL: So is there **any** message on the screen?
PR: Yes, it says 'Do you have **any** other version of Opsys on your system?'
HL: And do you?
PR: No, I have **no** version of Opsys at all.
HL: So, press 'enter'.
PR: Now it says 'You have too **little** disk space for installation.'
HL: How **much** disk space does it say you have?
PR: 2.4 megabytes.
HL: Then you'll have to delete **a few** programs to make disk space. Do you have **many** backup files on your hard disk?
PR: Yes, I think I have **a lot.**
HL: Well, you don't need those. You can delete **all** of them.
PR: OK, I'll do that now. Can you wait **a little** while?
HL: Yes.
PR: Right, I've deleted **all** of them.
HL: So, now key in 'install' again and let's see if you can load Opsys.
PR: Right. Yes, it's working. Now it shows '25 per cent installed'.
HL: So, it's installed **a few** of the files.
PR: Now 50 per cent... now 75 per cent.
HL: Right, that's **most** of the files.
PR: Now 100 per cent.
HL: Good, so that's **all** of it installed.
PR: Thanks for your help.

UNIT 56

Exercise 1

1	c	2	b	3	b
4	a	5	b		

Exercise 2

It has come to our notice that a very **few** of the Tantra models sold over the last few months may have **a little** problem with their electrical wiring. We would like to emphasise that **most** of the products are defect-free and this problem affects only **a few** models. However, we have decided to recall **all** the Tantra models with serial numbers from A56000 to B12000. In **most** cases, you will find this number at the back of the machine; in the newer models it is on the side. Finally, let me reassure **all** our customers that this fault poses **no** danger whatever and we are recalling them merely as a precaution.

Exercise 3

1	c	2	e	3	d
4	a	5	f	6	b

UNIT 57

Exercise 1

E	V	E	R	Y	O	N	E	B	A	L	L
G	I	L	B	N	O	O	F	S	T	R	I
C	O	P	E	R	T	B	T	R	L	O	T
N	I	T	I	N	N	O	N	E	A	S	T
B	R	E	R	F	O	D	A	S	N	P	L
P	O	E	V	E	R	Y	W	H	E	R	E
N	U	A	R	W	Z	O	I	Y	V	A	R
M	U	C	H	F	R	U	I	T	E	T	R
R	M	H	O	P	S	E	V	E	R	A	L

Exercise 2

1 We have been selling our products **everywhere** in Europe for many years now.
2 **Each** of our European subsidiaries **has** been very successful in entering new markets.
3 **Everyone/Everybody** in our European offices **is** linked via a local area network.
4 **Each/Every** senior manager **receives** regular training in the latest management techniques.
5 I am very surprised that **every time** I visit head office, I meet new personnel.
6 We feel that we have carried out **everything** necessary to secure the future survival of the firm.
7 We prepare management accounts **every three months/every quarter.**
8 **Each** of our employees **is** encouraged to contribute to the suggestions scheme.

Exercise 3

1	d	2	f	3	b	4	e
5	g	6	a	7	c		

UNIT 58

Exercise 1

1 1,446
2 $3\frac{3}{4}$
3 85.762
4 23 April 1999; 23rd April 1999; 23.4.1999; 23/04/99
5 18.35; 6.35 p.m.
6 $1m
7 £5.7bn
8 8m × 4m
9 25 + 16 = 41
10 8^2
11 $\sqrt{8}$
12 9^{25}

Exercise 2

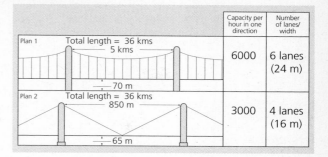

		Capacity per hour in one direction	Number of lanes/ width
Plan 1 Total length = 36 kms 5 kms 70 m		6000	6 lanes (24 m)
Plan 2 Total length = 36 kms 850 m 65 m		3000	4 lanes (16 m)

Exercise 3

1 Marketing meeting on 16th February at 14.00 in room 4. Call ext. 9346.
2 Brochure: A4 – 120 words/page; A4 + 3 cms – 150 words/page. Subheadings: ( ) or [ ]?
3 Delivery on 18 February after 09.00. Dimensions: 3.5 m wide × 2.8 m long × 30 cms deep. Ring 562731.
4 Marketing receipts: 120 francs + 2,600 ptas + 12,460 lire not = £516.

UNIT 59

Exercise 1

B	E	T	W	E	E	N
Y	E	G	X	Z	F	P
D	A	F	T	E	R	N
U	R	R	O	T	O	M
R	G	I	N	R	M	S
I	K	X	L	O	E	B
N	G	H	A	A	N	C
G	U	N	T	I	L	A

Exercise 2

'**Before** we can decide on a name for the product we shall have to commission some market research. It is important that we decide this **by** the **beginning** of January because **during** the whole of January we will be talking to an advertising agency about ideas on how to promote the product **in** time for the autumn season. **On** February 1, we will begin discussions on implementation of ideas. Then **between** March and July we will turn ideas into firm strategy. Everything will be ready **by** August 1 for the launch **in** September.'

UNIT 60

Exercise 1

During the 1970s the European car industry was in crisis. **After** several difficult years **throughout** the 1980s, with a lot of reorganisation and jobs lost, the industry changed dramatically. Not only were the major manufacturers in better economic and industrial health, but **from** the **beginning** of the 1990s cars were better designed and more reliable. One reason for this improvement was that **during** the 1980s there was strong competition from the Pacific Rim, and Japan in particular. The emphasis was on quality and reliability. **From** the early 1980s **to** the present, there has been a revolution in the performance of almost every manufacturer. Now there are still too many cars in production, but poor design and bad quality are a thing of the past.

Exercise 2

1 Wrong. **During** the night, there is little demand for power.
2 Wrong. Then **in** the morning, demand rises again as people wake up and make breakfast.
3 Wrong. **From** early morning to around midday, demand is constant, with an increase **at/around** lunchtime.
4 Wrong. **Throughout** the afternoon, demand is fairly constant **until** the evening when it increases as people get home from work.
5 Right.
6 Obviously **from** sundown **till/until** bedtime demand remains high, especially **in** winter.

UNIT 61

Exercise 1

Julia: So, what's your itinerary for your Latin American trip next week?

Brian: Well, it's very busy. **On** the first day, Monday, we land **in** Peru – we'll visit two customers **in** the Callao district of Lima, **near** the port. **After** two meetings with them we'll spend the night **in** Lima, meeting them again **on** Tuesday morning if necessary. If not we can relax and go **to** a museum, or have a look **at/around** the city centre, or simply wait **at/in** the hotel if we prefer.

Julia: It doesn't sound too busy so far!

Brian: Well, there's more to come! **On** Tuesday afternoon **at** three o'clock we take a plane **from** Lima **to** Arequipa **in** the south of Peru. Here we have our main agent for the Andean region, so we're going to spend two days with him. Then we take a plane **over** the Andes, direct **to** Buenos Aires to meet our Argentinian agent…

Julia: Is he in Buenos Aires?

Brian: Well, not exactly. But not **far away.** About thirty kilometres **from** the city centre, but I think he has an office **close** to the centre. But our meeting will be at his ranch – **outside** the city.

Julia: That sounds good! And when do you get back?

Brian: **On** May 23, **at** four o'clock in the morning!

Exercise 2

1	over	2	on top of	3	outside
4	under	5	through	6	inside
7	into	8	away from	9	along
10	at	11	to	12	across
13	on	14	off		

UNIT 62

Exercise 1

1 Right.
2 Wrong. We arrived **in** Los Angeles **on** a Sunday evening.
3 Wrong. We stayed **at** the Hotel Excelsior.
4 Right.
5 Right.
6 Wrong. We then went up to San Francisco and stayed **at** a friend's house.
7 Wrong. We stayed there **(for)** a week.
8 Wrong. At the end of the week we decided to go **to** Arizona.
9 Wrong. We had to drive **across** the Nevada desert.
10 Wrong. It was incredibly hot under the Nevada sun **at/around** midday.
11 Wrong. We spent two weeks **in** Arizona.
12 Right.
13 Wrong. We drove to Las Vegas and flew home **from** there.

Exercise 2

The gas turbine engine works by air passing **through** its four main parts. First cold air enters the compressor (1). The compressor reduces the air pressure and forces air **into** the heat exchanger (2). Hot exhaust combustion gases ensure that the temperature **inside** the heat exchanger remains high. The air is heated and then is forced **through** the combustion chamber (3). Fuel is burned **in** the combustion chamber, raising the temperature to 650°C. These gases are then forced **out** of the combustion chamber and **into** the turbine (4). This drives the turbine.

UNIT 63

Exercise 1

1 I'll see you **at** the beginning of the month.
2 I'm away now **for** a few days.
3 He takes a day off **on** Christmas Day.
4 He takes three days off **at** Easter.
5 I live **in** an apartment.
6 The repair will take _____ a week.
7 I'll see you **in** the hotel lobby.
8 Do you mean **at** reception?
9 The film begins **at** 10 o'clock.
10 Is the presentation **in** the main auditorium?
11 No, you should go **to** Room 48.
12 He used to live **near/close to/by** the sea.
13 He had a house **on** an island.
14 I like walking **around** beautiful cities.
15 I prefer walking **on/along** deserted beaches.
16 I was born **in** 1956 **on** December 30.
17 Shakespeare came **from** Stratford-on-Avon **in** England.
18 Without a visa you can't get **into** the country.
19 Without an export licence, you can't send some goods **out of** the country.

20 Some people can't sleep **at** night after drinking coffee.
21 Then they fall asleep **during** the day.
22 I'm going _____ home now.
23 **In** three months we move **into/to** a new office.
24 Can I borrow this book **until/till** next week?
25 I'll give it **(to)** you **(on)** Monday.
26 We won't meet _____ tomorrow. I'll see you _____ next week.

Exercise 2

Diana: **Before** breakfast I'd like to have a swim.
Anna: Really?
Diana: Yes, of course! Then **over** breakfast we can meet our colleagues **from** Paris. **In** the morning we should have a brainstorm to identify key areas of interest.
Anna: Yes, I think so too.
Diana: **By** lunchtime we should have an agenda for the afternoon. Then we should go **to** a restaurant for lunch. **At** two o'clock we should begin the afternoon session.
Anna: Okay. Sounds okay.
Diana: I think we'll finish **around** four o'clock. So, see you **at** breakfast. Good night!

UNIT 64

Exercise 1

| 1 E | 2 S | 3 L/A |
| 4 S | 5 E | 6 SIM |

Exercise 2

In the petroleum industry, a key area of the drilling operation is known **as** mud technology. Mud, sometimes known **as** drilling fluid, in the petroleum engineering context, is not **like** mud for the gardener. Mud is often a complex combination of ingredients used to circulate throughout the bore-hole, or drill-hole, during drilling. The mud works **as** a lubricant with several other important functions, **such as** the following: it cleans out the bore-hole, returns pieces of rock to the surface, protects the sides of the bore-hole, preventing problems **such as** the sides caving in, it lubricates and cools the bit and maintains steady air pressure. Different muds are used for different conditions. Chemicals are added to the mud so that it sets **like** jelly when not being pumped, so avoiding problems **such as** the bore-hole getting blocked up.

Usually one individual works **as** a Mud Engineer, someone who is responsible for controlling the behaviour of the mud and checking that the drilling operation works **as** it should. This is a key responsibility since, **as** already stated, mud is a complex and vitally important aspect of the industry.

Exercise 3

As you know, we need to employ people who have worked **as** top-level research scientists. Salaries have to be **as** high **as** those in other companies **like** ours.

People **like** Tom do not understand the competition we face in recruiting top people, **such as** the candidate he thinks is too expensive.

UNIT 65

Exercise 1

1	a	two different areas: new systems and modification of existing systems
	b	four types of service: new systems, custom-built designs, system modification and consultancy
2	a	clearly
	b	first of all, secondly, at first, subsequently
	c	briefly, to sum up
	d	on the whole

Exercise 2

The International Trade division of the bank offers two main **categories** of service. These are consultancy services and financial services. The consultancy services sector is **divided into** three: these are firstly economic information, **secondly** status enquiries and **finally** a trade development service. Now, the other category of service is financial services. This **consists of** three **kinds.** The **first** is acceptance credit, then there is buyer credit and **lastly** there's foreign currency loans.

UNIT 66

Exercise 1

1 f	2 i	3 a
4 e	5 b	6 g
7 h	8 c	9 d

Exercise 2

J: So, first of all, can you say how the products you sell are categorised?
M: Yes, it's quite simple. We have two basic product **categories,** food and non-food items.
J: And what does each category **consist** of?
M: Basically, food items **comprises** four classes: groceries, meat, perishables and drinks. And **under** non-food items we have healthcare and cosmetics, household goods and clothing.
J: What sort of things are **included** under household goods?
M: There are three **basic** types: kitchenware, paper goods and cleaning materials. And then under perishables, we have dairy products and foods sold on the delicatessen. Meat is **divided** into three kinds: fresh meat, frozen meat and fish.

UNIT 67

Exercise 1

Exercise 2

1 **Vice-President (Marketing)** – term used in American English.
2 **Company Director** – term used in British English.
3 **Production Manager** – managerial position, the others are not.
4 **Human Resources Director** – same as 3.

Exercise 3

I: Who actually **runs** the University?
DCA: Well, the Academic Board, **headed by** the Vice-Chancellor, is the governing body.
I: Who sits on the Board?
DCA: There are three Directors. Each **reports** to the Vice-Chancellor. They **manage** the three main areas of activity, Finance, Academic Affairs and Corporate Affairs.
I: What about the different Faculties, where do they **come in?**
DCA: The Faculties **come under** the Director of Academic Affairs. He is also **responsible for** the Registry and International Partnerships.

UNIT 68

Exercise 1

1 **raise** – it is transitive.
2 **shrink** – means to reduce or get smaller.
3 **peak** – means the highest point.
4 **slight** – means not very much.
5 **slump** – this is a noun or verb, not a modifier.
6 **fluctuation** – means rapid rising and falling.

Exercise 2

1	b	2	a	3	d
4	f	5	c	6	e

Exercise 3

'We can see how differently the three products have performed. Firstly, Product A has shown a **continual** climb in sales and now **stands** at $5000 per year. In contrast, five years ago Product B had sales of over $3000 but since then has not **increased.** But the performance of Product B is still good, having more or less **remained constant** over the five-year period. Now, let's compare these with Product C which shows the most **dramatic** trend, **rising** from $2000 five years ago to reach a peak of almost $5000 in the

fourth year before beginning a **sudden** decline to its present level of just $1000, a **reduction** that is practically a complete **collapse.**'

UNIT 69

Exercise 1

1	d	2	f	3	e
4	c	5	a	6	b

Exercise 2

I: Can you describe the trend in world water use over the century?
O: Well, for 60 years, industrial and domestic use of water was insignificant, **whereas** agricultural use was relatively high even in 1900. **However,** suddenly there was a huge increase in domestic use and **even more** for industrial use. **In spite of** this, the real shock comes when we look at agricultural use. This is now up to three times **greater** than industrial use and it is still increasing dramatically. **While** all three types of use are increasing, agricultural use is positively rocketing.

Exercise 3

1 Proposal 1 involves a Commercial Vehicle Division which, in terms of status, **is similar to** the Cars Division.
2 **On the other hand** Proposal 2 **is different** in that Cars appears to **correspond to** PSV or Agricultural Vehicles.
3 In reality Cars accounts for 50 per cent of our business, so Proposal 1 **resembles** the actual situation **more closely.**
4 **In spite of** this objection, the Board prefers Proposal 2.

UNIT 70

Exercise 1

1 I don't think that's possible.
2 I'm sure that's out of the question.
3 We clearly won't have an easy time.
4 The report suggests there are problems.

Exercise 2

Assertive
It's quite obvious that the test was badly designed.
That's totally impossible – we spent three months planning it.
It doesn't matter if you spent three years on it.
Neutral
I think we should call another meeting.
Shall we ask the R&D team to send a representative?
Yes, that's a good idea.
Downtoning
I wonder if we ought to bring in some outside experts.
It might be a good idea to see if we have the money for that.
Whatever we do, I'm inclined to think costs will limit our actions.

Exercise 3 (M)

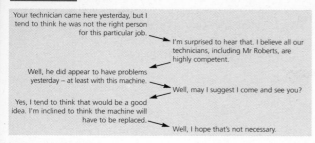

Your technician came here yesterday, but I tend to think he was not the right person for this particular job.

I'm surprised to hear that. I believe all our technicians, including Mr Roberts, are highly competent.

Well, he did appear to have problems yesterday – at least with this machine.

Well, may I suggest I come and see you?

Yes, I tend to think that would be a good idea. I'm inclined to think the machine will have to be replaced.

Well, I hope that's not necessary.

UNIT 71

Exercise 1 (M)

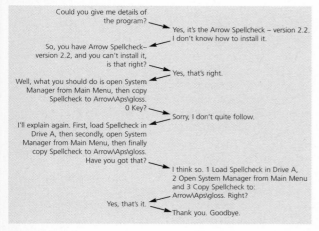

Could you give me details of the program?

Yes, it's the Arrow Spellcheck – version 2.2. I don't know how to install it.

So, you have Arrow Spellcheck– version 2.2, and you can't install it, is that right?

Yes, that's right.

Well, what you should do is open System Manager from Main Menu, then copy Spellcheck to Arrow\Aps\gloss. 0 Key?

Sorry, I don't quite follow.

I'll explain again. First, load Spellcheck in Drive A, then secondly, open System Manager from Main Menu, then finally copy Spellcheck to Arrow\Aps\gloss. Have you got that?

I think so. 1 Load Spellcheck in Drive A, 2 Open System Manager from Main Menu and 3 Copy Spellcheck to: Arrow\Aps\gloss. Right?

Yes, that's it.

Thank you. Goodbye.

Exercise 2

E: An unfavourable labour market is threatening the prospects for economic recovery in many sectors of the economy.

J: Could you **explain in more detail** what that means?

E: Well, labour costs and a highly regulated employment market make unit labour costs much higher than in competitor economies.

J: **Are you saying** wages are too high?

E: Certainly that's true. But other factors contribute to labour costs, such as insurance costs, equal pay laws, restrictive working practices, health and safety conditions.

J: So, **in other words** a whole range of social legislation is responsible for labour costs.

E: Yes. All this, **as I've already said,** makes labour very expensive.

J: So, **to paraphrase what you've said,** high labour costs and a restrictive labour market are damaging the prospects for recovery?

E: That's it. I believe so.

UNIT 72

Exercise 1

T: Can we fix a meeting soon?

M: Yes, when **would you like to meet?**

T: **I'd rather it were** early next month.

M: Hmm. I think that should be okay, but **I'd prefer** a Monday.

T: That's no problem. Now, where? Where **would you prefer?** Your office or mine?

M: **I'd rather meet** in a beautiful holiday resort, Bermuda for example!

T: Yes, Bermuda's great. But **I'd like to come to** your office. **I prefer your** coffee. Also, **I like going** to that French restaurant round the corner.

Exercise 2

A: Where <u>do</u> **(would)** you usually stay, in a family-run hotel or in a big chain hotel like this one?

P: I <u>prefer</u> **(to)** <u>stay</u> in a big chain hotel, because when I'm on business I only think about work. When I travel with my family, then I <u>am liking</u> **(like)** a more personal hotel.

A: So you don't go out to the theatre or enjoy yourself when you're on business?

P: Actually, I rarely go the theatre. I <u>like more</u> **(prefer)** music, so I go to concerts.

A: Yes, so do I. <u>Do you like</u> **(Would you like to)** go to a concert this evening?

P: <u>I</u> **(I'd)** like that, but unfortunately I have a meeting this evening. But what's the concert?

A: It's an evening of Mozart at the City Hall.

P: That would be good, but I have to say I prefer <u>more</u> **( )** Beethoven.

A: I think I do too. Let me get you a drink. What <u>do</u> **(would)** you like?

P: I'd like <u>that I have</u> **( )** an apple juice.

Exercise 3

A: Would you **like** to see a copy of the report before the meeting?

B: Yes, I'd **prefer to see** it as soon as possible.

A: Do you **want** me to come to the meeting?

B: I'd **prefer** you didn't come.

A: That's fine. I'd **rather** stay away.

UNIT 73

Exercise 1 (M)

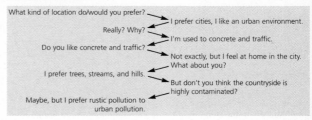

What kind of location do/would you prefer?

I prefer cities, I like an urban environment.

Really? Why?

I'm used to concrete and traffic.

Do you like concrete and traffic?

Not exactly, but I feel at home in the city. What about you?

I prefer trees, streams, and hills.

But don't you think the countryside is highly contaminated?

Maybe, but I prefer rustic pollution to urban pollution.

Exercise 2 (M)

1 I'm inclined to think the rural location will mean higher transport costs.

2 Relocation might create domestic problems for our staff.

3 It could be that a lot of people will work from home.

4 Isn't it true that working from home also creates domestic problems?

5 I tend to think we shouldn't move – the costs could be enormous.

Exercise 3 (M)

Obviously, we should reconsider the decision.
We **really** cannot do this without everyone's support.
There is **clearly** a danger that we have chosen the wrong location.
We **definitely** have to look at all the drawbacks again.
Evidently, the decision to move is in the best interests of the company.

UNIT 74

Exercise 1

A: So I'd **like to** ask you what you **think** about this research problem.
B: My **view/feeling** is that we **should/must** take on a new Research Officer.
A: You **could** be right, **but** we have to think about the costs.
C: I'm sorry, I **can't agree** with Ben. I **really** think we already have enough people in Research.

Exercise 2 (M)

MD: So, I'm concerned about the quality of communication here in Logicam. <u>I was wondering what your views might be on</u> (1) how we operate, in the area of communication processes. You've no doubt got a lot of experience in this…
MM: <u>Well, I'm not sure I have a lot, I've only been here six months</u>… (6)
MD: … but you have expertise and experience in other companies and, more importantly, you see Logicam with fresh eyes. <u>What do you think of communication here?</u> (2)
MM: Well, <u>I'm sure it could be improved</u> (3) and I know people complain… you know, too much paper, poor use of IT…
MD: So, <u>do you have any suggestions?</u> (2) How can we improve things?
MM: Well, first of all <u>I think I'd recommend</u> (4) a communications audit, you know, an assessment of the situation, find out what happens, what people think.
MD: Yes, <u>I'm sure you're right</u>. (5) I was thinking along those lines. Could you do that?
MM: Well, no, I don't have much expertise in this area, but also, I think it would be better if we used an outsider, someone independent, not directly involved.
MD: <u>Yes, I can see the advantages there.</u> (5) So, a consultant then?
MM: Yes, but they'd need to get to know us. Or a combination, someone from inside the company, together with a consultant.
MD: <u>That might be possible,</u> (5) a possible way. So, <u>you think it could be effective, like that?</u> (2)
MM: I think it could be, but <u>I'm inclined to think</u> (4) it would be a long process. Getting to know the company, making proposals, having discussions, making recommendations, implementing

decisions, auditing the results of implementation… so, a long project.
MD: Do you have anyone in mind?
MM: Yes, as it happens, my husband is a Communications Consultant…

UNIT 75

Exercise 1 (M)

1 a   Absolutely!
   b   You're probably right.
2 a   That's clear.
   b   Yes, I think you could be right.
3 a   We don't.
   b   Unfortunately, I'm inclined to agree.

Exercise 2 (M)

1 a   Of course we could!
   b   Are you sure?
2 a   I don't accept that. Why not?
   b   Actually, I feel we probably can.
3 a   He certainly isn't. Not Mr Roach!
   b   I'm afraid I don't altogether agree with you.

Exercise 3

A: So, what **do** you **think** about the Hurst plan?
B: I'm **inclined** to think it won't work.
A: Really? Surely you are being pessimistic?
B: I think we'd have problems.
A: What **kind** of problems?

A: The weakness in the plan is that it is not properly costed.
B: I'm sorry, I can't **accept** that. We costed every detail.
C: Yes, I think we did, but the costs are too high.
B: Yes, they are high, **but** on the other hand, I don't think we have any choice.

A: Henry thinks the insurance costs are too high.
H: No, I **didn't** say that. I simply said they *are* high.
B: Well, Henry, I don't think I **can/really** agree **with** you. In fact, they're reasonable.

A: Can I **ask** if anyone has any views on the price? Ben?
B: I **tend** to think it's okay.
C: Yes, it's okay, but I also think we **should** look at alternatives.
D: We've spent enough time on this already. We should go ahead.
C: No. We have to get it right.

A: That is a brilliant idea!
B: No it **isn't.** It'll **never** work.
A: You're **wrong.** You'll see.

Exercise 1

2 The shortage has **led** to a government decision to introduce restrictions on water.
3 The restrictions may **bring about** some financial savings.
4 Abuse of the restrictions may **give rise to** prosecutions.
5 In some areas, the restrictions on water use **cause** problems for industry.

Exercise 2

The city authority is concerned about the effect on the infrastructure of the city of large and increasing volumes of tourists. A recent report claims that high volume tourism is changing the character of the city centre.

Many businesses have moved away from the town centre because local people no longer enjoy shopping there. Also, the volume of visitors has resulted in damage to some historic monuments. For example, large numbers of visitors have affected some of the 700-year-old paintings in the Cathedral. In another example, coachloads of visitors to Liberation Park have resulted in a reduction in some species of bird life on the ponds.

---

memo

Subject: Growth in tourism
To: SS   From: IFT   Date: 21.9.96

Businesses have moved away because local people no longer shop in the city.

The volume of visitors has caused damage to monuments.

Large numbers of visitors have affected paintings in Cathedral.

Coachloads of visitors to the park have resulted in disturbance to the birds.

Exercise 3

1 The ship sank due to water entering the lower car deck.
2 Water entered the lower car deck as a consequence of an insecure bow door.
3 Because of poor working practices, the door was not closed properly.
4 Owing to inadequate supervision, there was frequently careless work.
5 The unreasonable hurry to leave the port area was attributable to commercial pressures.

Exercise 1 (M)

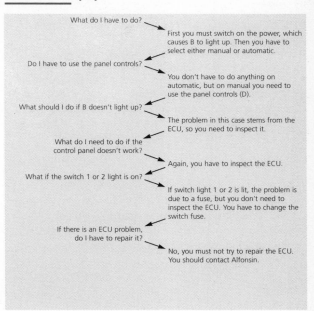

Exercise 2 (M)

1 If you move the switch **forward** it makes the platform go forward.
2 If you move the switch backwards, it **causes** the platform to go backwards.
3 Moving the switch to the left **results in** the platform going to the left.

Exercise 1

All financial service advisors, banks and building societies are now **required/obliged** by law to write to individual clients setting out the terms of their engagements. The new regulations **oblige/require** companies to give detailed descriptions of the work they are qualified to do. They are also **supposed** to specify all charges and commissions.

A further change is that all individuals working as advisors **need** to be fully qualified. Anyone without the necessary professional qualifications is **banned** from giving financial advice. As a result many individuals with years of experience will be **forced** to take professional examinations. Unqualified persons will no longer be **permitted** to give even informal advice.

Exercise 2

Obligation	No obligation	Obligation not to do something
1	3	4
2	5	
6		

UNIT 79

Exercise 1

1 Due to management ruling, **the use of Room 4 is banned.**
2 We regret this machine **is not capable of providing** all the goods you require.
3 The amount of electricity we may use **is restricted.**
4 We **are forced to withdraw** the credit facilities we have made available to you in the past.
5 **You do not need to/needn't** visit next week.
6 We **are compelled to** make major cost savings.

Exercise 2

The import of certain products which we have in the past obtained from you is no longer **permitted** since the introduction of tougher safety controls. I will send you a full list of the regulations as they affect your products.

In the meantime please note that we have stocks of certain products that we are **unable** to sell. Please tell us if you **can** take back these items. You may **be able** to modify them.

Please note the following:

1 attachments of the type used on TR396 are now **banned.**
2 we are **prohibited** from selling existing stock of TR431.
3 we are not **allowed** to sell TR397 on account of the metal ring.

UNIT 80

Exercise 1

1 d   2 c   3 e   4 b   5 a

Exercise 2

1 See italics below.
2 See underlined phrases below.
3 Optical fibre and laser equipment, linked to a monitor.
4 Sophisticated control mechanisms.
5 resulted in, resulting from, therefore, brought about.
6 enabled, can, allows, permit.

> Non-invasive surgery using fibre optic technology and laser beams has resulted in *considerable improvements in treatment for a range of conditions.* One of the many benefits resulting from these developments has been the *lower risk of infection* and *improved healing times. Patients are therefore able to leave hospital relatively quickly.* This has also brought about considerable *cost benefits* and enabled *more patients to be treated more quickly.*
>
> Non-invasive surgery means the surgeon can <u>perform operations on internal organs without having to make major incisions</u>. Optical fibre and laser equipment, linked to a monitor, allows the surgeon to <u>see a magnified image of the target tissue</u> in the body. Sophisticated control mechanisms permit delicate operations to be performed with minimum damage to surrounding tissue.

UNIT 81

Exercise 1

1 d   2 c   3 e
4 a   5 b

Exercise 2

It is quite **likely** that the world air travel market will see major changes in the near future. There is a problem of over-capacity, with many airlines **incapable** of increasing their market share. Smaller airlines are already largely **prevented** from operating on the most popular routes. There are **bound** to be more takeovers, as smaller airlines prove **unable** to compete.

Exercise 3

Dan Cavan, Chairman of Credit Bank International, said yesterday at the CBI Annual General Meeting, that it is almost **certain** that other banks, as well as his own, will try to take over Northern Bank. He claimed that last year the takeover of Northern Bank by CBI was considered **highly likely.** However, CBI was **unable** to persuade NB shareholders to accept the merger. Indeed, the NB board was **prevented from** continuing talks. He went on to say that now CBI may be in a **position** to make a better offer for Northern.

UNIT 82

Exercise 1 (M)

2 It's unlikely that PPS will increase its stake in European associate companies.
3 The company may improve its existing 14 per cent share of the global market.
4 It is quite probable that TriValve system will achieve record sales.
5 The new production plant in Seoul is sure to open this year.

Exercise 2

1 Given that he is very clever, it is **likely** that he will be successful.
2 I am certain that she **is** the best person to lead the team.
3 I'm **quite** certain that she will accept the appointment.
4 It is **highly probable** that we'll be successful so I'm bound to be optimistic.
5 We **are** bound to benefit from increased publicity.

Exercise 3

2 d   3 a   4 c

UNIT 83

Exercise 1

1 Why **don't** you call your agent?
2 I think you **should** speak to him as soon as possible.

3   I suggest **you/we** find out what the problem is.
4   We **ought** to have a decision on what to do.
5   If we can't decide, I **suggest** having another meeting next week.
6   No, **let's** solve the problem today.
7   How **about** having a short break?

Exercise 2

John Smith recommended getting our Legal Department to examine exactly how they are breaking the contract.

Carla V. suggested we should ask Arco for a meeting to discuss ways to resolve the problem.

Finally, Tom H. advised us to get independent legal advice.

In conclusion, it was agreed to meet again on Monday.

Exercise 3 (M)

Dear Brigitte,

I have been thinking about the problem you referred to when we spoke on the telephone on Monday. I'd like to make some suggestions.

I'd recommend you relocate Paul to a different office, or I'd suggest you eliminate the possibility of Paul having to take orders from Sam.

Alternatively, you should ask Personnel to move one of them to another department.

As a last resort, why not have a meeting with them to get them to change their attitude to one another.

UNIT 84

Exercise 1

1 (A) (IND)   3 (I) (IND)
2 (A) (D)   4 (A)
               5 (I) (D)

Exercise 2 (M)

Q: Can I ask if you have 100 2 kg packs of cheese and basil tortellini in stock?
A: Yes, no problem!
Q: Could you despatch them this morning for delivery later today?
A: Yes, but may I suggest the order is made by fax?
Q: No problem. Also, could you please send 20*l*. of Spanish olive oil?
A: Yes, of course.
Q: And can you tell me when the delivery will arrive?
A: Can I call you back to tell you?
Q: Yes, but if you don't mind, could you find out in the next 10 minutes?
A: Yes, I'll do that.

Exercise 3

1 e   4 b
2 d   5 a
3 c